Most Lawyers Are Liars

The Truth About Accounting

Written By

Money Guy and Tax Guy

Most Lawyers Are Liars - The Truth About Accounting

Copyright © 2022 by Money Guy and Tax Guy

All rights reserved. Published 2022

Published by Don't Read In The Dark Publishing |

For information about exclusive discounts for bulk purchases, please contact Don't Read in The Dark

Cover Design and Book Layout by: - Jake Sparks

Book Edited: Susan Lunsford

Money Guy Tax Guy

First Edition Print

ISBN: 1-939670-51-9

Printed in the USA.

Although the authors have made every effort to ensure that the information in this book was correct at press time, the author does not assume and hereby disclaims any liability to any party for any loss, damage, or disruption caused by errors or omissions, whether such errors or omissions result from negligence, accident, or any other cause. This is not financial or investment advice, while we might be tax and business consultants, we are not your tax and business consultants.

Welcome to the wonderful world of accounting. Most lawyers do not have a clue how to do accounting, let alone, understand why they need to do it We will tackle the terms, the reason, and the how it all works.

What Is Accounting?

Accounting is the process of recording financial transactions pertaining to a business. The accounting process includes summarizing, analyzing, and reporting these transactions to oversight agencies, regulators, and tax collection entities. The financial statements used in accounting are a concise summary of financial transactions over an accounting period, summarizing a company's operations, financial position, and cash flows.

Key Takeaways

- Regardless of the size of a business, accounting is a necessary function for decision making, cost planning, and measurement of economic performance measurement.

- A bookkeeper can manage basic accounting needs, but a Certified Public Accountant (CPA) should be utilized for larger or more advanced accounting tasks.

- Two important types of accounting for businesses are managerial accounting and cost accounting. Managerial accounting helps management teams make business decisions, while cost accounting helps business owners decide how much a product should cost.

- Professional accountants follow a set of standards known as the Generally Accepted Accounting Principles (GAAP) when preparing financial statements.

Accounting

How Accounting Works

Accounting is one of the key functions of almost any business. It may be managed by a bookkeeper or an accountant at a small firm, or by sizable finance departments with dozens of employees at larger companies. The reports generated by various streams of accounting, such as cost accounting and managerial accounting, are invaluable in helping management make informed business decisions.

The financial statements that summarize a large company's operations, financial position, and cash flows over a particular period are concise and consolidated reports based on thousands of individual financial transactions. As a result, all accounting designations are the culmination of years of study and rigorous examinations combined with a minimum number of years of practical accounting experience.

While basic accounting functions can be handled by a bookkeeper, advanced accounting is typically handled by qualified accountants who possess designations such as Certified Public Accountant (CPA) or Certified Management Accountant (CMA) in the United States. In Canada, the three legacy designations—the Chartered Accountant (CA), Certified General Accountant (CGA), and Certified Management Accountant (CMA)—have been unified under the Chartered Professional Accountant (CPA) designation.

The Alliance for Responsible Professional Licensing (ARPL) was formed in August 2019 in response to a series of state deregulatory proposals making the requirements to become a CPA more lenient. The ARPL is a coalition of various advanced professional groups including engineers, accountants, and architects.

Types of Accounting

Financial Accounting

Financial accounting refers to the processes used to generate interim and annual financial statements. The results of all financial transactions that occur during an accounting period are summarized into the balance sheet, income statement, and cash flow statement. The financial statements of most companies are audited annually by an external CPA firm. For some, such as publicly traded companies, audits are a legal requirement. However, lenders also typically require the results of an external audit annually as part of their debt covenants. Therefore, most companies will have annual audits for one reason or another.

Managerial Accounting

Managerial accounting uses much of the same data as financial accounting, but it organizes and utilizes information in different ways. Namely, in managerial accounting, an accountant generates monthly or quarterly reports that a business's management team can use to make decisions about how the business operates. Managerial accounting also encompasses many other facets of accounting, including budgeting, forecasting, and various financial analysis tools. Any information that may be useful to management falls underneath this umbrella.

Cost Accounting

Just as managerial accounting helps businesses make decisions about management, cost accounting helps businesses make decisions about costing. Cost accounting considers all the costs related to producing a product. Analysts, managers, business owners, and accountants use this information to determine what their products should cost. In cost accounting, money is cast as an economic factor in production, whereas in financial accounting, money is a measure of a company's economic performance.

Requirements for Accounting

In most cases, accountants use generally accepted accounting principles (GAAP) when preparing financial statements in the U.S. GAAP is a set of standards and principles designed to improve the comparability and consistency of financial reporting across industries. Its standards are based on double-entry accounting, a method in which every accounting transaction is entered as both a debit and credit in two separate general ledger accounts that will roll up into the balance sheet and income statement.

In most other countries, a set of standards governed by the International Accounting Standards Board named the International Financial Reporting Standards (IFRS) is used.

Example of Accounting

To illustrate double-entry accounting, imagine a business sends an invoice to one of its clients. An accountant using the double-entry method records a debit to accounts receivables, which flows through to the balance sheet, and a credit to sales revenue, which flows through to the income statement.

When the client pays the invoice, the accountant credits accounts receivables and debits cash. Double-entry accounting is also called balancing the books, as all the accounting entries are balanced against each other. If the entries aren't balanced, the accountant knows there must be a mistake somewhere in the general ledger.

History of Accounting

The history of accounting has been around as long as money itself. Accounting history dates to ancient civilizations in Mesopotamia, Egypt, and Babylon. For example, during the Roman Empire, the government had detailed records of its finances. However, modern accounting as a profession has only been around since the early 19th century.

Luca Pacioli is considered "The Father of Accounting and Bookkeeping" due to his contributions to the development of accounting as a profession. An Italian mathematician and friend of Leonardo da Vinci, Pacioli published a book on the double-entry system of bookkeeping in 1494.

By 1880, the modern profession of accounting was fully formed and recognized by the Institute of Chartered Accountants in England and Wales. This institute created many of the systems by which accountants practice today. The formation of the institute occurred in large part due to the Industrial Revolution. Merchants not only needed to track their records but sought to avoid bankruptcy as well.

What Is Accounting?

Accounting is a profession whose core responsibility is to help businesses maintain accurate and timely records of their finances. Accountants are responsible for maintaining records of a company's daily transactions and compiling those transactions into financial statements such as the balance sheet, income statement, and statement of cash flows. Accountants also provide other services, such as performing periodic audits or preparing ad-hoc management reports.

What Skills Are Required for Accounting?

Accountants hail from a wide variety of backgrounds. However, diligence is a key component in accountancy since accountants must be able to diagnose and correct subtle errors or discrepancies in a company's accounts. The ability to think logically is also essential, to help with problem-solving. Mathematical skills are helpful but are less important than in previous generations due to the wide availability of computers and calculators.

Why Is Accounting Important for Investors?

The work performed by accountants is at the heart of modern financial markets. Without accounting, investors would be unable to rely on timely or accurate financial information, and companies' executives would lack the transparency needed to manage risks or plan projects. Regulators also rely on accountants for critical functions such as providing auditors' opinions on companies' annual 10-K filings. In short, although accounting is sometimes overlooked, it is critical for the smooth functioning of modern finance.

Accounting Equation

What Is the Accounting Equation?

The accounting equation states that a company's total assets are equal to the sum of its liabilities and its shareholders' equity.

This straightforward number on a company balance sheet is the foundation of the double-entry accounting system. The accounting equation ensures that the balance sheet remains balanced. That is, each entry made on the debit side has a corresponding entry (or coverage) on the credit side.

The accounting equation is also called the basic accounting equation or the balance sheet equation.

Key Takeaways

- The accounting equation is the foundation of the double-entry accounting system.

- The accounting equation shows on a company's balance that a company's total assets are equal to the sum of the company's liabilities and shareholders' equity.

- Assets represent the valuable resources controlled by the company. The liabilities represent their obligations.

- Both liabilities and shareholders' equity represent how the assets of a company are financed.

- Financing through debt shows as a liability, while financing through issuing equity shares appears in shareholders' equity.

Accounting Equation

Understanding the Accounting Equation

The financial position of any business, large or small, is based on two key components of the balance sheet: assets and liabilities. Owners' equity, or shareholders' equity, is the third section of the balance sheet.

The accounting equation is a representation of how these three important components are associated with each other.

Assets represent the valuable resources controlled by the company, while liabilities represent its obligations. Both liabilities and shareholders' equity represent how the assets of a company are financed. If it's financed through debt, it'll show as a liability, but if it's financed through issuing equity shares to investors, it'll show in shareholders' equity.

The accounting equation helps to assess whether the business transactions conducted by the company are being accurately reflected in its books and accounts. Below are examples of items listed on the balance sheet.

Assets

Assets include cash and cash equivalents or liquid assets, which may include Treasury bills and certificates of deposit.

Accounts receivables list the amounts of money owed to the company by its customers for the sale of its products.

Inventory is also considered an asset.

Liabilities

Liabilities are debts that a company owes and costs that it needs to pay to keep the company running.

Debt is a liability, whether it is a long-term loan or a bill that is due to be paid.

Costs include rent, taxes, utilities, salaries, wages, and dividends payable.

Shareholders' Equity

The shareholders' equity number is a company's total assets minus its total liabilities.

It can be defined as the total number of dollars that a company would have left if it liquidated all its assets and paid off all its liabilities. This would then be distributed to the shareholders.

Retained earnings are part of shareholders' equity. This number is the sum of total earnings that were not paid to shareholders as dividends.

Think of retained earnings as savings, since it represents the total profits that have been saved and put aside (or "retained") for future use.

Accounting Equation Formula and Calculation

Assets = (Liabilities + Owner's Equity) {Assets}={Liabilities} + {Owner's Equity} Assets = (Liabilities + Owner's Equity)

The balance sheet holds the elements that contribute to the accounting equation:

1. Locate the company's total assets on the balance sheet for the period.

2. Total all liabilities, which should be a separate listing on the balance sheet.

3. Locate total shareholder's equity and add the number to total liabilities.

4. Total assets will equal the sum of liabilities and total equity.

As an example, say the leading retailer XYZ Corporation reported the following on its balance sheet for its latest full fiscal year:

- Total assets: $170 billion

- Total liabilities: $120 billion

- Total shareholders' equity: $50 billion

If we calculate the right-hand side of the accounting equation (equity + liabilities), we arrive at ($50 billion + $120 billion) = $170 billion, which matches the value of the assets reported by the company.

About the Double-Entry System

The accounting equation is a concise expression of the complex, expanded, and multi-item display of a balance sheet.

The representation equates all uses of capital (assets) to all sources of capital, were debt capital leads to liabilities and equity capital leads to shareholders' equity.

For a company keeping accurate accounts, every business transaction will be represented in at least two of its accounts. For instance, if a business takes a loan from a bank, the borrowed money will be reflected in its balance sheet as both an increase in the company's assets and an increase in its loan liability.

If a business buys raw materials and pays in cash, it will result in an increase in the company's inventory (an asset) while reducing cash capital (another asset). Because there are two or more accounts affected by every transaction conducted by a company, the accounting system is referred to as double-entry accounting.

The double-entry practice ensures that the accounting equation always remains balanced, meaning that the left side value of the equation will always match the right-side value.

In other words, the total amount of all assets will always equal the sum of liabilities and shareholders' equity.

The global adherence to the double-entry accounting system makes the account keeping and tallying processes more standardized and more fool-proof.

The accounting equation ensures that all entries in the books and records are vetted, and a verifiable relationship exists between each liability (or expense) and its corresponding source; or between each item of income (or asset) and its source.

Limits of the Accounting Equation

Although the balance sheet always balances out, the accounting equation cannot tell investors how well a company is performing. Investors must interpret the numbers and decide for themselves whether the company has too many or too few liabilities, not enough assets, or too many assets, or whether its financing is sufficient to ensure its long-term growth.

Real World Example

Below is a portion of Exxon Mobil Corporation's (XOM) balance sheet in millions as of Dec. 31, 2019:

- Total assets were $362,597

- Total liabilities were $163,659

- Total equity was $198,938

The accounting equation is calculated as follows:

- Accounting equation = $163,659 (total liabilities) + $198,938 (equity) equals $362,597, (which equals the total assets for the period)

Why Is the Accounting Equation Important?

The accounting equation captures the relationship between the three components of a balance sheet: assets, liabilities, and equity.

A company's equity will increase when its assets increase, and vice-versa. Adding liabilities will decrease equity while reducing liabilities—such as by paying off debt—will increase equity.

These basic concepts are essential to modern accounting methods.

What Are the 3 Elements of the Accounting Equation?

The three elements of the accounting equation are assets, liabilities, and shareholders' equity.

The formula is straightforward: A company's total assets are equal to its liabilities plus its shareholders' equity.

The double-entry bookkeeping system, which has been adopted globally, is designed to accurately reflect a company's total assets.

What Is an Asset in the Accounting Equation?

An asset is anything with economic value that a company controls that can be used to benefit the business now or in the future.

They include fixed assets such as buildings and plants. They may include financial assets, such as investments in stocks and bonds. They also may be intangible assets like patents, trademarks, and goodwill.

What Is a Liability in the Accounting Equation?

A company's liabilities include every debt it has incurred. These may include loans, accounts payable, mortgages, deferred revenues, bond issues, warranties, and accrued expenses.

What Is Shareholders' Equity in the Accounting Equation?

Shareholders' equity is the total value of the company expressed in dollars.

Put another way, it is the amount that would remain if the company liquidated all its assets and paid off all its debts. The remainder is the shareholders' equity, which would be returned to them.

Asset

What Is an Asset?

An asset is a resource with economic value that an individual, corporation, or country owns or controls with the expectation that it will provide a future benefit. Assets are reported on a company's balance sheet and are bought or created to increase a firm's value or benefit the firm's operations. An asset can be thought of as something that, in the future, can generate cash flow, reduce expenses, or improve sales, regardless of whether it is manufacturing equipment or a patent.

Key Takeaways

- An asset is a resource with economic value that an individual, corporation, or country owns or controls with the expectation that it will provide a future benefit.

- Assets are reported on a company's balance sheet and are bought or created to increase a firm's value or benefit the firm's operations.

- An asset can be thought of as something that, in the future, can generate cash flow, reduce expenses, or improve sales, regardless of whether it is manufacturing equipment or a patent.

Asset

Understanding Assets

An asset represents an economic resource for a company or represents access that other individuals or firms do not have. A right or other access is legally enforceable, which means economic resources can be used at a company's discretion, and their use can be precluded or limited by an owner.

For an asset to be present, a company must possess a right to it as of the date of the financial statements. An economic resource is something that is scarce and can produce economic benefit by generating cash inflows or decreasing cash outflows.

Assets can be broadly categorized into short-term (or current) assets, fixed assets, financial investments, and intangible assets.

Types of Assets

Current Assets

Current assets are short-term economic resources that are expected to be converted into cash within one year. Current assets include cash and cash equivalents, accounts receivable, inventory, and various prepaid expenses.

While cash is easy to value, accountants periodically reassess the recoverability of inventory and accounts receivable. If there is evidence that accounts receivable might be uncollectible, it will become impaired. Or if inventory becomes obsolete, companies may write off these assets.

Assets are recorded on companies' balance sheets based on the concept of historical cost, which represents the original cost of the asset, adjusted for any improvements or aging.

Fixed Assets

Fixed assets are long-term resources, such as plants, equipment, and buildings. An adjustment for the aging of fixed assets is made based on periodic charges called depreciation, which may or may not reflect the loss of earning powers for a fixed asset.

Accepted accounting principles (GAAP) allow depreciation under two broad methods. The straight-line method assumes that a fixed asset loses its value in proportion to its useful life, while the accelerated method assumes that the asset loses its value faster in its first years of use.

Financial Assets

Financial assets represent investments in the assets and securities of other institutions. Financial assets include stocks, sovereign and corporate bonds, preferred equity, and other hybrid securities. Financial assets are valued depending on how the investment is categorized and the motive behind it.

Intangible Assets

Intangible assets are economic resources that have no physical presence. They include patents, trademarks, copyrights, and goodwill. Accounting for intangible assets differs depending on the type of asset, and they can be either amortized or evaluated for impairment each year.

How do I know if something is an asset?

An asset is something that provides a current, future, or potential economic benefit for an individual or other entity. An asset is, therefore, something that is owned by you or something that is owed to you. Therefore, a $10 bill, a desktop computer, a chair, or a car are all assets. If somebody owes you money, that loan is also an asset because you are owed that amount (even though the loan is a liability for the one paying you back).

What about non-physical assets?

Intangible assets provide an economic benefit to somebody, but you cannot physically touch them. These are an important class of assets that include things like intellectual property (e.g., patents or trademarks), contractual obligations, royalties, and goodwill. Brand equity and reputation are also examples of non-physical assets that can be quite valuable. Some financial assets, such as shares of stock or derivatives contracts are also intangible.

Is labor an asset?

No. Labor is the work conducted by human beings, for which they are paid in wages or a salary. Labor is distinct from assets, which are capital.

How are current assets different from fixed (noncurrent) assets?

Companies will segregate their assets by their time horizon in use. Fixed assets, also known as noncurrent assets, are intended for longer-term use (one year or longer) and are not often easily liquidated. As a result, unlike current assets, fixed assets undergo depreciation.

Liability Definition
What Is a Liability?

A liability is something a person or company owes, usually a sum of money. Liabilities are settled over time through the transfer of economic benefits including money, goods, or services. Recorded on the right side of the balance sheet, liabilities include loans, accounts payable, mortgages, deferred revenues, bonds, warranties, and accrued expenses.

Key Takeaways

- A liability (speaking) is something that is owed to somebody else.

- Liability can also mean a legal or regulatory risk or obligation.

- In accounting, companies book liabilities in opposition to assets.

- Current liabilities are a company's short-term financial obligations that are due within one year or a normal operating cycle (e.g., accounts payable).

- Long-term (non-current) liabilities are obligations listed on the balance sheet not due for more than a year.

What's a Liability?

How Liabilities Work

In general, a liability is an obligation between one party, and another not yet completed or paid for. In the world of accounting, a financial liability is also an obligation but is more defined by previous business transactions, events, sales, exchange of assets or services, or anything that would provide economic benefit at a later date. Current liabilities are usually considered short-term (expected to be concluded in 12 months or less) and non-current liabilities are long-term (12 months or greater).

Liabilities are categorized as current or non-current depending on their temporality. They can include a future service owed to others (short- or long-term borrowing from banks, individuals, or other entities) or a previous transaction that has created an unsettled obligation. The most common liabilities are usually the largest like accounts payable and bonds payable. Most companies will have these two-line items on their balance sheet, as they are part of ongoing current and long-term operations.

Liabilities are a vital aspect of a company because they are used to finance operations and pay for large expansions. They can also make transactions between businesses more efficient. For example, in most cases, if a wine supplier sells a case of wine to a restaurant, it does not demand payment when it delivers the goods. Rather, it invoices the restaurant for the purchase to streamline the drop-off and make paying easier for the restaurant.

The outstanding money that the restaurant owes to its wine supplier is considered a liability. In contrast, the wine supplier considers the money it is owed to be an asset.

Liability may also refer to the legal liability of a business or individual. For example, many businesses take out liability insurance in case a customer or employee sues them for negligence.

Other Definitions of Liability

Liability refers to the state of being responsible for something, and this term can refer to any money or service owed to another party. Tax liability, for example, can refer to the property taxes that a homeowner owes to the municipal government or the income tax he owes to the federal government. When a retailer collects sales tax from a customer, they have a sales tax liability on their books until they remit those funds to the county/city/state.

Types of Liabilities

Businesses sort their liabilities into two categories: current and long-term. Current liabilities are debts payable within one year, while long-term liabilities are debts payable over a longer period. For example, if a business takes out a mortgage payable over a 15-year period, that is a long-term liability. However, the mortgage payments that are due during the current year are considered the current portion of long-term debt and are recorded in the short-term liabilities section of the balance sheet.

Current Liabilities

Ideally, analysts want to see that a company can pay current liabilities, which are due within a year, with cash. Some examples of short-term liabilities include payroll expenses and accounts payable, which include money owed to vendors, monthly utilities, and similar expenses. Other examples include:

- Wages Payable: The total amount of accrued income employees have earned but not yet received. Since most companies pay their employees every two weeks, this liability changes often.

- Interest Payable: Companies, just like individuals, often use credit to purchase goods and services to finance over brief time periods. This represents the interest on those short-term credit purchases to be paid.

- Dividends Payable: For companies that have issued stock to investors and pay a dividend, this represents the amount owed to shareholders after the dividend was declared. This period is around two weeks, so this liability usually pops up four times per year, until the dividend is paid.

- Unearned Revenues: This is a company's liability to deliver goods and/or services at a future date after being paid in advance. This amount will be reduced in the future with an offsetting entry once the product or service is delivered.

- Liabilities of Discontinued Operations: This is a unique liability that most people glance over but should scrutinize more closely. Companies are required to account for the budgetary impact of an operation, division, or entity that is currently being held for sale or has been recently sold. This also includes the budgetary impact of a product line that is or has recently been shut down.

Non-Current Liabilities

Considering the name, it is obvious that any liability that is not current falls under non-current liabilities expected to be paid in 12 months or more. Referring again to the AT&T example, there are more items than your garden variety company that may list one or two items. Long-term debt, also known as bonds payable, is usually the largest liability and at the top of the list.

Companies of all sizes finance part of their ongoing long-term operations by issuing bonds that are loans from each party that purchases the bonds. This line item is in constant flux as bonds are issued, mature, or called back by the issuer.

Analysts want to see that long-term liabilities can be paid with assets derived from future earnings or financing transactions. Bonds and loans are not the only long-term liabilities companies incur. Items like rent, deferred taxes, payroll, and pension obligations can also be listed under long-term liabilities. Other examples include:

- Warranty Liability: Some liabilities are not as exact as AP and must be estimated. It is the estimated amount of time and money that may be spent repairing products upon the agreement of a warranty. This is a common liability in the automotive industry, as most cars have long-term warranties that can be costly.

- Contingent Liability Evaluation: A contingent liability is a liability that may occur depending on the outcome of an uncertain future event.

- Deferred Credits: This is a broad category that may be recorded as current or non-current depending on the specifics of the transactions. These credits are revenue collected before it being earned and recorded on the income statement. It may include customer advances, deferred revenue, or a transaction where credits are owed but not yet considered revenue. Once the revenue is no longer deferred, this item is reduced by the amount earned and becomes part of the company's revenue stream.

- Post-Employment Benefits: These are benefitting an employee or family members may receive upon his/her retirement, which are carried as a long-term liability as it accrues. In the AT&T example, this constitutes one-half of the total non-current total second only to long-term debt. With rapidly rising health care and deferred compensation, this liability is not to be overlooked.

- Unamortized Investment Tax Credits (UITC): This represents the net between an asset's historical cost and the amount that has already been depreciated. The unamortized portion is a liability, but it is only a rough estimate of the asset's fair market value. For an analyst, this provides some details of how aggressive or conservative a company is with its depreciation methods.

Liabilities vs. Assets

Assets are the things a company owns—or things owed to the company—and they include tangible items such as buildings, machinery, and equipment as well as intangible items such as accounts receivable, interest owed, patents, or intellectual property.

If a business subtracts its liabilities from its assets, the difference is its owner's or stockholders' equity. This relationship can be expressed as follows:

Assets− Liabilities = Owner's Equity {Assets}-{Liabilities} = {Owner's Equity} Assets−Liabilities=Owner's Equity

However, in most cases, this accounting equation is commonly presented as such:

Assets = Liabilities + Equity {Assets} = {Liabilities} + {Equity}Assets = Liabilities + Equity

Liabilities vs. Expenses

An expense is the cost of operations that a company incurs to generate revenue. Unlike assets and liabilities, expenses are related to revenue, and both are listed on a company's income statement. In short, expenses are used to calculate net income. The equation to calculate net income is revenues minus expenses.

For example, if a company has more expenses than revenues for the past three years, it may signal weak financial stability because it has been losing money for those years.

Expenses and liabilities should not be confused with each other. One is listed on a company's balance sheet, and the other is listed on the company's income statement. Expenses are the costs of a company's operation, while liabilities are the obligations and debts a company owes. Expenses can be paid immediately with cash, or the payment could be delayed which would create a liability.

Example of Liabilities

As a practical example of understanding a firm's liabilities, let's look at a historical example using AT&T's (T) 2020 balance sheet.1 The current/short-term liabilities are separated from long-term/non-current liabilities on the balance sheet.

AT&T clearly defines its bank debt that is maturing in less than one year under current liabilities. For a company this size, this is often used as operating capital for day-to-day operations rather than funding larger items, which would be better suited using long-term debt.

Like most assets, liabilities are carried at cost, not market value, and under generally accepted accounting principle (GAAP) rules can be listed in order of preference as long as they are categorized. The AT&T example has a high debt level under current liabilities. With smaller companies, other line items like accounts payable (AP) and various future liabilities like payroll, taxes will be higher current debt obligations.

AP typically carries the largest balances, as they encompass the day-to-day operations. AP can include services, raw materials, office supplies, or any other categories of products and services where no promissory note is issued. Since most companies do not pay for goods and services as they are acquired, AP is equivalent to a stack of bills waiting to be paid.

How Do I Know If Something Is a Liability?

A liability is something that is owed to or obligated to someone else. It can be real (e.g., a bill that needs to be paid) or potential (e.g., a lawsuit).

How Are Current Liabilities Different from Long-Term (Noncurrent) Ones?

Companies will segregate their liabilities by their time horizon for when they are due. Current liabilities are due with a year and are often paid for using current assets. Non-current liabilities are due in more than one year and most often include debt repayments and deferred payments.

How Do Liabilities Relate to Assets and Equity?

The accounting equation states that—assets = liabilities + equity. As a result, we can re-arrange the formula to read liabilities = assets - equity. Thus, the value of a firm's total liabilities will equal the difference between the values of total assets and shareholders' equity. If a firm takes on more liabilities without accumulating additional assets, it must result in a reduction in the value of the firm's equity position.

What Is a Contingent Liability?

A contingent liability is an obligation that might have to be paid in the future, but there are still unresolved matters that make it only a possibility and not a certainty. Lawsuits and the threat of lawsuits are the most common contingent liabilities, but unused gift cards, product warranties, and recalls also fit into this category.

What Are Examples of Liabilities That Individuals or Households Have?

Like businesses, an individual's or household's net worth is taken by balancing assets against liabilities. For most households, liabilities will include taxes due, bills that must be paid, rent or mortgage payments, loan interest and principal due, and so on. If you are pre-paid for performing work or a service, the work owed may also be construed as a liability.

Equity
What Is Equity?

Equity, typically referred to as shareholders' equity (or owners' equity for privately held companies), represents the amount of money that would be returned to a company's shareholders if all the assets were liquidated, and all the company's debt was paid off in the case of liquidation. In the case of acquisition, it is the value of company sales minus any liabilities owed by the company not transferred with the sale.

In addition, shareholder equity can represent the book value of a company. Equity can sometimes be offered as payment-in-kind. It also represents the pro-rata ownership of a company's shares.

Equity can be found on a company's balance sheet and is one of the most common pieces of data employed by analysts to assess the financial health of a company.

Key Takeaways

- Equity represents the value that would be returned to a company's shareholders if all the assets were liquidated, and all the company's debts were paid off.

- We can also think of equity as a degree of residual ownership in a firm or asset after subtracting all debts associated with that asset.

- Equity represents the shareholders' stake in the company, identified on a company's balance sheet.

- The calculation of equity is a company's total assets minus its total liabilities and is used in several key financial ratios such as ROE.

Equity

Formula and Calculation for Shareholder Equity

The following formula and calculation can be used to determine the equity of a firm, which is derived from the accounting equation:

Shareholders' Equity=Total Assets−Total Liabilities {Shareholders' Equity} = {Total Assets} - {Total Liabilities} Shareholders' Equity=Total Assets−Total Liabilities

This information can be found on the balance sheet, where these four steps should be followed:

1. Locate the company's total assets on the balance sheet for the period.

2. Locate total liabilities, which should be listed separately on the balance sheet.

3. Subtract total liabilities from total assets to arrive at shareholder equity.

4. Note that total assets will equal the sum of liabilities and total equity.

Shareholder equity can also be expressed as a company's share capital and retained earnings less the value of treasury shares. This method, however, is less common. Though both methods yield the same figure, the use of total assets and total liabilities is more illustrative of a company's financial health.

Understanding Shareholder Equity

By comparing concrete numbers reflecting everything the company owns and everything it owes, the "assets-minus-liabilities" shareholder equity equation paints a clear picture of a company's finances, which can be easily interpreted by investors and analysts. Equity is used as capital raised by a company, which is then used to purchase assets, invest in projects, and fund operations. A firm typically can raise capital by issuing debt (in the form of a loan or via bonds) or equity (by selling stock). Investors typically seek out equity investments as it provides greater opportunity to share in the profits and growth of a firm.

Equity is important because it represents the value of an investor's stake in a company, represented by their proportion of the company's shares. Owning stock in a company gives shareholders the potential for capital gains as well as dividends. Owning equity will also give shareholders the right to vote on corporate actions and in any elections for the board of directors. These equity ownership benefits promote shareholders' ongoing interest in the company.

Shareholder equity can be either negative or positive. If positive, the company has enough assets to cover its liabilities. If negative, the company's liabilities exceed its assets; if prolonged, this is considered balance sheet insolvency. Typically, investor's view companies with negative shareholder equity as risky or unsafe investments. Shareholder equity alone is not a definitive indicator of a company's financial health; used in conjunction with other tools and metrics, the investor can accurately analyze the health of an organization.

Components of Shareholder Equity

Retained earnings are part of shareholder equity and are the percentage of net earnings that were not paid to shareholders as dividends. Think of retained earnings as savings since it represents a cumulative total of profits that have been saved and put aside or retained for future use. Retained earnings grow larger over time as the company continues to reinvest a portion of its income.

At some point, the amount of accumulated retained earnings can exceed the amount of equity capital contributed by stockholders. Retained earnings are usually the largest component of stockholders' equity for companies that have been operating for many years.

Treasury shares or stock (not to be confused with U.S. Treasury bills) represent stock that the company has bought back from existing shareholders. Companies may do a repurchase when management cannot deploy all the available equity capital in ways that might deliver the best returns. Shares bought back by companies become treasury shares, and their dollar value is noted in an account called treasury stock, a contra account to the accounts of investor capital and retained earnings. Companies can reissue treasury shares back to stockholders when companies need to raise money.

Many view stockholders' equity as representing a company's net assets—its net value would be the amount shareholders would receive if the company liquidated all its assets and repaid all its debts.

Example of Shareholder Equity

Using a historical example, below is a portion of Exxon Mobil Corporation's (XOM) balance sheet as of September 30, 2018:

- Total assets were $354,628 (highlighted in green).

- Total liabilities were $157,797 (1st highlighted red area).

- Total equity was $196,831 (2nd highlighted red area).

The accounting equation whereby assets = liabilities + shareholder equity is calculated as follows:

Shareholder equity = $354,628, (total assets) - $157,797 (total liabilities) = $196,831

Other Forms of Equity

The concept of equity has applications beyond just evaluating companies. We can more generally think of equity as a degree of ownership in any asset after subtracting all debts associated with that asset.

Below are several common variations on equity:

- A stock or any other security representing an ownership interest in a company.

- On a company's balance sheet, the amount of the funds contributed by the owners or shareholders plus the retained earnings (or losses). One may also call this stockholders' equity or shareholders' equity.

- In margin trading, the value of securities in a margin account minus what the account holder borrowed from the brokerage.

- In real estate, the difference between the property's current fair market value and the amount the owner still owes on the mortgage. It is the amount that the owner would receive after selling a property and paying any liens. Also referred to as "real property value."

- When a business goes bankrupt and has to liquidate, equity is the amount of money remaining after the business repays its creditors. This is most often called "ownership equity," also known as risk capital or "liable capital."

Private Equity

When an investment is publicly traded, the market value of equity is readily available by looking at the company's share price and its market capitalization. For private entitles, the market mechanism does not exist, and so other forms of valuation must be done to estimate value.

Private equity refers to such an evaluation of companies that are not publicly traded. The accounting equation still applies where stated equity on the balance sheet is what is left over when subtracting liabilities from assets, arriving at an estimate of book value. Privately held companies can then seek investors by selling off shares directly in private placements. These private equity investors can include institutions like pension funds, university endowments, and insurance companies, or accredited individuals.

Private equity is often sold to funds and investors that specialize in direct investments in private companies or that engage in leveraged buyouts (LBOs) of public companies. In an LBO transaction, a company receives a loan from a private equity firm to fund the acquisition of a division of another company. Cash flows or the assets of the company being acquired usually secure the loan. Mezzanine debt is a private loan, usually provided by a commercial bank or a mezzanine venture capital firm. Mezzanine transactions often involve a mix of debt and equity in the form of a subordinated loan or warrants, common stock, or preferred stock.

Private equity comes into play at different points along a company's life cycle. Typically, a young company with no revenue or earnings can't afford to borrow, so it must get capital from friends and family or individual "angel investors." Venture capitalists enter the picture when the company has finally created its product or service and is ready to bring it to market. Some of the largest, most successful corporations in the tech sector, like Google, Apple, Facebook, and Amazon—or what is referred to as Big Techs or GAFAM— all began with venture capital funding.

Venture capitalists (VCs) provide most private equity financing in return for an early minority stake. Sometimes, a venture capitalist will take a seat on the board of directors for its portfolio companies, ensuring an active role in guiding the company. Venture capitalists look to hit big early on and exit investments within five to seven years. An LBO is one of the most common types of private equity financing and might occur as a company matures.

A final type of private equity is a Private Investment in a Public Company (PIPE). A PIPE is a private investment firms, a mutual fund's, or another qualified investors' purchase, of stock in a company at a discount to the current market value (CMV) per share, to raise capital.

Unlike shareholder equity, private equity is not accessible for the average individual. Only "accredited" investors, those with a net worth of at least $1 million, can take part in private equity or venture capital partnerships. Such endeavors might require the use of form 4, depending on their scale. For investors who have do not meet this marker, there is the option of exchange-traded funds (ETFs) that focus on investing in private companies.

Equity Begins at Home

Home equity is comparable to the value contained in homeownership. The amount of equity one has in their residence represents how much of the home that they own outright by subtracting from it the mortgage debt owed. Equity on a property or home stems from payments made against a mortgage, including a down payment, and from increases in property value.

Home equity is often an individual's greatest source of collateral, and the owner can use it to get a home equity loan, which some call a second mortgage or a home equity line of credit (HELOC). Taking money out of a property or borrowing money against it is an equity takeout.

For example, let us say Sam owns a home with a mortgage on it. The house has a current market value of $175,000 and the mortgage owed totals $100,000. Sam has $75,000 worth of equity in the home or $175,000 (asset total) - $100,000 (liability total).

Brand Equity

When determining an asset's equity, particularly for larger corporations, it is important to note these assets may include both tangible assets, like property, and intangible assets, like the company's reputation and brand identity. Through years of advertising and development of a customer base, a company's brand can come to have an inherent value. Some call this value "brand equity," which measures the value of a brand relative to a generic or store-brand version of a product.

For example, many soft-drink lovers will reach for a Coke before buying a store-brand cola because they prefer the taste or are more familiar with the flavor. If a 2-liter bottle of store-brand cola costs $1 and a 2-liter bottle of Coke costs $2, then The Coca-Cola has brand equity of $1.

There is also such a thing as negative brand equity, which is when people will pay more for a generic or store-brand product than they will for a particular brand name. Negative brand equity is rare and can occur because of bad publicity, such as a product recall or a disaster.

Equity vs. Return on Equity

Return on equity (ROE) is a measure of financial performance calculated by dividing net income by shareholder equity. Because shareholder equity is equal to a company's assets minus its debt, ROE could be thought of as the return on net assets. ROE is considered a measure of how effectively management is using a company's assets to create profits.

Equity, as we have seen, has various meanings but usually represents ownership in an asset or a company such as stockholders owning equity in a company. ROE is a financial metric that measures how much profit is generated from a company's shareholder equity.

What exactly is equity?

Equity is an important concept in finance that has different specific meanings depending on the context. The most common type of equity is "shareholders' equity," which is calculated by taking a company's total assets and subtracting its total liabilities.

Shareholders' equity is, therefore, the net worth of a corporation. If the company were to liquidate, shareholders' equity is the amount of money that would theoretically be received by its shareholders.

What are some other terms used to describe equity?

Other terms that are sometimes used to describe this concept include shareholders' equity, book value, and net asset value. Depending on the context, the precise meanings of these terms may differ, but they refer to the value of an investment that would be left over after paying off all the liabilities associated with that investment. This term is also used in real estate investing to refer to the difference between a property's reasonable value and the outstanding value of its mortgage loan.

How is equity used by investors?

Equity is an especially important concept for investors. For instance, in looking at a company, an investor might use shareholders' equity as a benchmark for determining whether a particular purchase price is high. If that company has historically traded at a price to book value of 1.5, for instance, then an investor might think twice before paying more than that valuation unless they feel the company's prospects have fundamentally improved. On the other hand, an investor might feel comfortable buying shares in a weak business as long as the price they pay is sufficiently low relative to its equity.

Revenue
What Is Revenue?

Revenue is the money generated from normal business operations, calculated as the average sales price times the number of units sold. It is the top line (or gross income) figure from which costs are subtracted to determine net income. Revenue is also known as sales on the income statement.

Key Takeaways

- Revenue, often referred to as sales or the top line, is the money received from normal business operations.

- Operating income is revenue (from the sale of goods or services) fewer operating expenses.

- Non-operating income is infrequent or nonrecurring income derived from secondary sources (e.g., lawsuit proceeds).

What is Revenue?

Understanding Revenue

Revenue is money brought into a company by its business activities. There are diverse ways to calculate revenue, depending on the accounting method employed. Accrual accounting will include sales made on credit as revenue for goods or services delivered to the customer.

It is necessary to check the cash flow statement to assess how efficiently a company collects money owed. Cash accounting, on the other hand, will only count sales as revenue when payment is received. Cash paid to a company is known as a "receipt." It is possible to have receipts without revenue. For example, if the customer paid in advance for a service not yet rendered or undelivered goods, this activity leads to a receipt but not revenue.

Revenue is known as the top line because it appears first on a company's income statement. Net income, also known as the bottom line, is revenues minus expenses. There is a profit when revenues exceed expenses.

To increase profit, and hence earnings per share (EPS) for its shareholders, a company increases revenues and/or reduces expenses. Investors often consider a company's revenue and net income separately to determine the health of a business. Net income can grow while revenues remain stagnant because of cost-cutting.

Such a situation does not bode well for a company's long-term growth. When public companies report their quarterly earnings, two figures that receive a lot of attention are revenues and EPS. A company beating or missing analysts' revenue and earnings per share expectations can often move a stock's price.

Revenue is also known as sales, as in the price-to-sales (P/S) ratio—an alternative to the price-to-earnings (P/E) ratio that uses revenue in the denominator.

Types of Revenue

A company's revenue may be subdivided according to the divisions that generate it. For example, a recreational vehicles department might have a financing division, which could be a separate source of revenue.

Revenue can also be divided into operating revenue—sales from a company's core business—and non-operating revenue which is derived from secondary sources. As these non-operating revenue sources are often unpredictable or nonrecurring, they can be referred to as one-time events or gains. For example, proceeds from the sale of an asset, a windfall from investments, or money awarded through litigation are non-operating revenue.

Examples of Revenue

In the case of government, revenue is the money received from taxation, fees, fines, inter-governmental grants or transfers, securities sales, mineral or resource rights, as well as any sales made.

For non-profits, revenues are its gross receipts. Its components include donations from individuals, foundations, and companies; grants from government entities; investments; fundraising activities; and membership fees.

In terms of real estate investments, revenue refers to the income generated by a property, such as rent or parking fees. When the operating expenses incurred in running the property are subtracted from property income, the resulting value is net operating income (NOI).

Are Revenue and Cash Flow the Same Thing?

No. Revenue is the money a company earns from the sale of its products and services. Cash flow is the net amount of cash being transferred into and out of a company. Revenue provides a measure of the effectiveness of a company's sales and marketing, whereas cash flow is more of a liquidity indicator. Both revenue and cash flow should be analyzed together for a comprehensive review of a company's financial health.

How Does One Generate Revenue?

For many companies, revenues are generated from the sales of products or services. For this reason, revenue is sometimes known as gross sales. Revenue can also be earned via other sources. Inventors or entertainers may receive revenue from licensing, patents, or royalties. Real estate investors might earn revenue from rental income.

Revenue for federal and local governments would be in the form of tax receipts from property or income taxes. Governments might also earn revenue from the sale of an asset or interest income from a bond. Charities and non-profit organizations usually receive income from donations and grants. Universities could earn revenue from charging tuition but also from investment gains on their endowment fund.

What Is Accrued and Deferred Revenue?

Accrued revenue is the revenue earned by a company for the delivery of goods or services that have yet to be paid by the customer. In accrual accounting, revenue is reported at the time a sales transaction takes place and may not necessarily represent cash in hand.

Deferred, or unearned revenue can be thought of as the opposite of accrued revenue, in that unearned revenue accounts for money prepaid by a customer for goods or services that have yet to be delivered. If a company has received prepayment for its goods, it would recognize the revenue as unearned, but would not recognize the revenue on its income statement until the period for which the goods or services were delivered.

Can a Company Have Positive Revenue but Negative Profit?

Yes. A company has a cost to produce goods sold, as well as other fixed costs and obligations like taxes and interest payments due on loans. As a result, if total costs exceed revenues, a company will have a negative profit even though it may be bringing in a lot of money from sales.

Expense
What is an Expense?

An expense is the cost of operations that a company incurs to generate revenue. As the popular saying goes, "it costs money to make money."

Common expenses include payments to suppliers, employee wages, factory leases, and equipment depreciation. Businesses are allowed to write off tax-deductible expenses on their income tax returns to lower their taxable income and thus their tax liability. However, the Internal Revenue Service (IRS) has strict rules on which expenses business are allowed to claim as a deduction.

Key Takeaways

- An expense is the cost of operations that a company incurs to generate revenue.

- Businesses can write off tax-deductible expenses on their income tax returns if they meet the IRS' guidelines.

- Accountants record expenses through one of two accounting methods: cash basis or accrual basis.

- There are two main categories of business expenses in accounting: operating expenses and non-operating expenses.

- The IRS treats capital expenses differently than most other business expenses.

Operating Expenses

Understanding Expenses

One of the main goals of company management teams is to maximize profits. This is achieved by boosting revenues while keeping expenses in check. Slashing costs can help companies to make even more money from sales.

However, if expenses are cut too much it could also have a detrimental effect. For example, paying less on advertising reduces costs but also lowers the company's visibility and ability to reach out to potential customers.

How Expenses Are Recorded

Companies break down their revenues and expenses in their income statements. Accountants record expenses through one of two accounting methods: cash basis or accrual basis. Under cash basis accounting, expenses are recorded when they are paid. In contrast, under the accrual method, expenses are recorded when they are incurred.

For example, if a business owner schedules a carpet cleaner to clean the carpets in the office, a company using cash basis records the expense when it pays the invoice. Under the accrual method, the business accountant would record the carpet cleaning expense when the company receives the service. Expenses are recorded on an accrual basis, ensuring that they match up with the revenues reported in accounting periods.

Expenses are used to calculate net income. The equation to calculate net income is revenues minus expenses.

Two Types of Business Expenses

There are two main categories of business expenses in accounting:

- Operating expenses: Expenses related to the company's main activities, such as the cost of goods sold, administrative fees, and rent.

- Non-operating expenses: Expenses not related to the business' core operations. Common examples include interest charges and other costs associated with borrowing money.

Special Considerations

Capital Expenses

Capital expenditures, commonly known as CapEx, are funds used by a company to acquire, upgrade, and maintain physical assets such as property, buildings, an industrial plant, technology, or equipment.

The IRS treats capital expenses differently than most other business expenses. While most costs of doing business can be expensed or written off against business income the year they are incurred, capital expenses must be capitalized or written off slowly over time.

The IRS has a schedule that dictates the portion of a capital asset a business may write off each year until the entire expense is claimed. The number of years over which a business writes off a capital expense varies based on the type of asset.

Not All Expenses Can Be Deducted

According to the IRS, to be deductible, a business expense "must be both ordinary and necessary." Ordinary means the expense is common or accepted in that industry, while necessarily means the expense is helpful in the pursuit of earning income. Business owners are not allowed to claim their personal, non-business expenses as business deductions. They also cannot claim lobbying expenses, penalties, and fines.

Investors can refer to Publication 535, Business Expenses on the IRS website for more information.

How Current and Noncurrent Assets Differ
Current: think short; noncurrent: think long

In financial accounting, assets are the resources that a company requires to run and grow its business. Assets are divided into two categories: current and noncurrent assets, which appear on a company's balance sheet and combine to form a company's total assets.

Understanding Short and Long-Term Assets

You may think of current assets as short-term assets, which are necessary for a company's immediate needs; whereas noncurrent assets are long-term, as they have a useful life of more than a year.

Current Assets: Short-Term

Current assets are considered short-term assets because they are convertible to cash within a firm's fiscal year and are the resources that a company needs to run its day-to-day operations and pay its current expenses. Current assets are reported on the balance sheet at their current or market price.

Current assets may include items such as:

- Cash and cash equivalents

- Accounts receivable

- Prepaid expenses

- Inventory

- Marketable securities

Cash and equivalents (that may be converted) may be used to pay a company's short-term debt. Accounts receivable consist of the expected payments from customers to be collected within one year. Inventory is also a current asset because it includes raw materials and finished goods that can be sold quickly.

Another important current asset for any business is inventories. It is important for a company to maintain a certain level of inventory to run its business, but neither high nor low levels of inventory are desirable. Other current assets can include deferred income taxes and prepaid revenue.

Noncurrent Assets: Long-Term

Noncurrent assets are a company's long-term investments that have a useful life of more than one year. Noncurrent assets cannot be converted to cash easily. They are required for the long-term needs of a business and include things like land and heavy equipment.

Noncurrent assets are reported on the balance sheet at the price a company paid for them, which is adjusted for depreciation and amortization and is subject to being re-evaluated whenever the market price decreases compared to the book price.

Noncurrent assets may include items such as:

- Land

- Property, plant, and equipment (PP&E)

- Trademarks

- Long-term investments and goodwill—when a company acquires another company

Noncurrent assets may be subdivided into tangible and intangible assets—such as fixed and intangible assets.

Fixed assets include property, plant, and equipment because they are tangible, meaning that they are physical in nature; we may touch them. A company cannot liquidate its PP&E easily. For example, an auto manufacturer's production facility would be labeled a noncurrent asset.

Intangible assets are nonphysical assets, such as patents and copyrights. They are considered as noncurrent assets because they provide value to a company but cannot be readily converted to cash within a year. Long-term investments, such as bonds and notes, are also considered noncurrent assets because a company usually holds these assets on its balance sheet for more than a year.

How Current and Noncurrent Assets Differ: A Quick Look

Current Assets

- Equal to cash or will be converted into cash within a year

- Used to fund immediate or current needs

- Items like cash and cash equivalents, short term investments, accounts receivables, inventories

- Valued at market prices

-

- Tax implications: Selling current assets results in the profit from trading activities

- Current assets not subject to revaluation—though in certain cases, inventories subject to revaluation

Noncurrent Assets

- Will not be converted into cash within one year

- Used to fund long-term or future needs

- Items like long term investments, PP&E, goodwill, depreciation and amortization, long-term deferred taxes assets

- Valued at cost less depreciation

- Tax implications: Selling assets results in capital gains and capital gains tax is applied

- Common revaluation of PP&E—for instance, when the market value of a tangible asset decreases compared to the book value, a firm needs to revalue that asset

Accounting Theory
What Is Accounting Theory?

Accounting theory is a set of assumptions, frameworks, and methodologies used in the study and application of financial reporting principles. The study of accounting theory involves a review of both the historical foundations of accounting practices, as well as the way in which accounting practices are changed and added to the regulatory framework that governs financial statements and financial reporting.

Key Takeaways

- Accounting theory provides a guide for effective accounting and financial reporting.

- Accounting theory involves the assumptions and methodologies used in financial reporting, requiring a review of accounting practices and the regulatory framework.

- The Financial Accounting Standards Board (FASB) issues accepted accounting principles (GAAP) which aim to improve comparability and consistency in accounting information.

- Accounting theory is a continuously evolving subject, and it must adapt to new ways of doing business, new technological standards, and gaps that are discovered in reporting mechanisms.

Understanding Accounting Theory

All theories of accounting are bound by the conceptual framework of accounting. This framework is provided by the Financial Accounting Standards Board (FASB), an independent entity that works to outline and establish the key objectives of financial reporting by businesses, both public and private.1 Further, accounting theory can be thought of as the logical reasoning that helps evaluate and guide accounting practices. Accounting theory, as regulatory standards evolve, also helps develop new accounting practices and procedures.

Accounting theory is more qualitative than quantitative, in that it is a guide for effective accounting and financial reporting.

The most important aspect of accounting theory is usefulness. In the corporate finance world, this means that all financial statements should provide important information that can be used by financial statement readers to make informed business decisions. This also means that accounting theory is intentionally flexible so that it can produce effective financial information, even when the legal environment changes.

In addition to usefulness, accounting theory states that all accounting information should be relevant, dependable, comparable, and consistent. What this means is that all financial statements need to be accurate and adhere to U.S. generally accepted accounting principles (GAAP). Adherence to GAAP allows the preparation of financial statements to be both consistent to a company's past financials and comparable to the financials of other companies.

Finally, accounting theory requires that all accounting and financial professionals operate under four assumptions. The first assumption states that a business is a separate entity from its owners or creditors.

The second affirms the belief that a company will continue to exist and not go bankrupt. The third assumes that all financial statements are prepared with dollar amounts and not with other numbers like units of production. Finally, all financial statements must be prepared on a monthly or annual basis.

Special Considerations

Accounting as a discipline has existed since the 15th century. Since then, both businesses and economies have evolved. Accounting theory is a continuously evolving subject, and it must adapt to new ways of doing business, new technological standards, and gaps that are discovered in reporting mechanisms.

For example, organizations such as the International Accounting Standards Board help create and revise practical applications of accounting theory through modifications to their International Financial Reporting Standards (IFRS). Professionals such as Certified Public Accountants (CPAs) help companies navigate new and established accounting standards.

Accounting Principles
What Are Accounting Principles?

Accounting principles are the rules and guidelines that companies must follow when reporting financial data. The Financial Accounting Standards Board (FASB) issues a standardized set of accounting principles in the U.S. referred to as generally accepted accounting principles (GAAP).

Key Takeaways

- Accounting standards are implemented to improve the quality of financial information reported by companies.

- In the United States, the Financial Accounting Standards Board (FASB) issues Generally Accepted Accounting Principles (GAAP).

- GAAP is required for all publicly traded companies in the U.S.; it is also routinely implemented by non-publicly traded companies as well.

- Internationally, the International Accounting Standards Board (IASB) issues International Financial Reporting Standards (IFRS).

- The FASB and IASB sometimes work together to issue joint standards on hot-topic issues, but there is no intention for the U.S. to switch to IFRS soon.

Accounting Principles

Understanding Accounting Principles

The goal of any set of accounting principles is to ensure that a company's financial statements are complete, consistent, and comparable. This makes it easier for investors to analyze and extract useful information from the company's financial statements, including trend data over a period. It also facilitates the comparison of financial information across different companies. Accounting principles also help mitigate accounting fraud by increasing transparency and allowing red flags to be identified.

Generally Accepted Accounting Principles (GAAP)

Publicly traded companies in the United States are required to regularly file generally accepted accounting principles, or GAAP-compliant financial statements in order to remain publicly listed on stock exchanges. Chief officers of publicly traded companies and their independent auditors must certify that the financial statements and related notes were prepared in accordance with GAAP.

Some of the most fundamental accounting principles include the following:

- Accrual principle

- Conservatism principle

- Consistency principle

- Cost principle

- Economic entity principle

- Full disclosure principle

- Going concern principle

- Matching principle

- Materiality principle

- Monetary unit principle

- Reliability principle

- Revenue recognition principle

- Time period principle

GAAP helps govern the world of accounting by standardizing and regulating the definitions, assumptions, and methods used by accountants across the country. There are a number of principles, but some of the most notable include the revenue recognition principle, matching principle, materiality principle, and consistency principle. The goal of standardized accounting principles is to allow financial statement users to view a company's financials with certainty that the information disclosed in the report is complete, consistent, and comparable.

Completeness is ensured by the materiality principle, as all material transactions should be accounted for in the financial statements. Consistency refers to a company's use of accounting principles over time. When accounting principles allow a choice between multiple methods, a company should apply the same accounting method over time or disclose its change in accounting method in the footnotes to the financial statements.

Comparability is the ability for financial statement users to review multiple companies' financials side by side with the guarantee that accounting principles have been followed to the same set of standards. Accounting information is not absolute or concrete, and standards such as GAAP are developed to minimize the negative effects of inconsistent data. Without GAAP, comparing financial statements of companies would be extremely difficult, even within the same industry, making an apples-to-apples comparison hard. Inconsistencies and errors would also be harder to spot.

Privately held companies and nonprofit organizations may also be required by lenders or investors to file GAAP-compliant financial statements. For example, annual audited GAAP financial statements are a common loan covenant required by most banking institutions. Therefore, most companies and organizations in the United States comply with GAAP, even though it is not necessarily a requirement.

International Financial Reporting Standards (IFRS)

Accounting principles differ from country to country. The International Accounting Standards Board (IASB) issues International Financial Reporting Standards (IFRS). These standards are used in over 120 countries, including those in the European Union (EU). The Securities and Exchange Commission (SEC), the U.S. government agency responsible for protecting investors and maintaining order in the securities markets, has expressed that the U.S. will not be switching to IFRS in the foreseeable future. However, the FASB and the IASB continue to work together to issue similar regulations on certain topics as accounting issues arise. For example, in 2014 the FASB and the IASB jointly announced new revenue recognition standards.

Since accounting principles differ across the world, investors should take caution when comparing the financial statements of companies from different countries. The issue of differing accounting principles is less of a concern in more mature markets. Still, caution should be used as there is still leeway for number distortion under many sets of accounting principles.

Who Sets Accounting Principles and Standards?

Various bodies are responsible for setting accounting standards. In the United States, GAAP is regulated by the Financial Accounting Standards Board (FASB). In Europe and elsewhere, the IFRS are established by the International Accounting Standards Board (IASB).

How Does IFRS Differ from GAAP?

IFRS is a standards-based approach that is used internationally, while GAAP is a rules-based system used primarily in the U.S. The IFRS is seen as a more dynamic platform that is regularly being revised in response to an ever-changing financial environment, while GAAP is more static.

Several methodological differences exist between the two systems. For instance, GAAP allows companies to use either the First in, First out (FIFO) or Last in, First out (LIFO) as an inventory cost method. LIFO, however, is banned under IFRS.

When Were Accounting Principles First Set Forth?

Standardized accounting principles date all the way back to the advent of double-entry bookkeeping in the 15th and 16th centuries that introduced a T-ledger with matched entries for assets and liabilities. Some scholars have argued that the advent of double-entry accounting practices during that time provided a springboard for the rise of commerce and capitalism. The American Institute of Certified Public Accountants and the New York Stock Exchange attempted to launch the first accounting standards to be used by firms in the United States in the 1930s.

What Are Some Critiques of Accounting Principles?

Critics of principles-based accounting systems say they can give companies far too much freedom and do not prescribe transparency. They believe because companies do not have to follow specific rules that have been set out, their reporting may provide an inaccurate picture of their financial health. In the case of rules-based methods like GAAP, complex rules can cause unnecessary complications in the preparation of financial statements. These critics claim having strict rules means that companies must spend an unfair amount of their resources to comply with industry standards.

Accounting Standard
What Is an Accounting Standard?

An accounting standard is a common set of principles, standards, and procedures that define the basis of financial accounting policies and practices.

Key Takeaways

- An accounting standard is a common set of principles, standards, and procedures that define the basis of financial accounting policies and practices.

- Accounting standards apply to the full breadth of an entity's financial picture, including assets, liabilities, revenue, expenses, and shareholders' equity.

- Banks, investors, and regulatory agencies, count on accounting standards to ensure information about a given entity is relevant and accurate.

GAAP

Understanding Accounting Standard

Accounting standards improve the transparency of financial reporting in all countries. In the United States, the Generally Accepted Accounting Principles form the set of accounting standards widely accepted for preparing financial statements. International companies follow the International Financial Reporting Standards (IFRS), which are set by the International Accounting Standards Board and serve as the guideline for non-U.S. GAAP companies reporting financial statements.

Generally Accepted Accounting Principles are heavily used among public and private entities in the United States. The rest of the world primarily uses IFRS. Multinational entities are required to use these standards. The IASB establishes and interprets the international communities' accounting standards when preparing financial statements.

Accounting standards relate to all aspects of an entity's finances, including assets, liabilities, revenue, expenses, and shareholders' equity. Specific examples of an accounting standard include revenue recognition, asset classification, allowable methods for depreciation, what is considered depreciable, lease classifications, and outstanding share measurement.

The American Institute of Accountants, which is now known as the American Institute of Certified Public Accountants, and the New York Stock Exchange attempted to launch the first accounting standards in the 1930s. Following this attempt came the Securities Act of 1933 and the Securities Exchange Act of 1934, which created the Securities and Exchange Commission. Accounting standards have also been established by the Governmental Accounting Standards Board for accounting principles for all state and local governments.

Accounting standards specify when and how economic events are to be recognized, measured, and displayed. External entities, such as banks, investors, and regulatory agencies, rely on accounting standards to ensure relevant and accurate information is provided about the entity. These technical pronouncements have ensured transparency in reporting and set the boundaries for financial reporting measures.

U.S. GAAP Accounting Standards

The American Institute of Certified Public Accountants developed, managed, and enacted the first set of accounting standards. In 1973, these responsibilities were given to the newly created Financial Accounting Standards Board. The Securities and Exchange Commission requires all listed companies to adhere to U.S. GAAP accounting standards in the preparation of their financial statements to be listed on a U.S. securities exchange.

Accounting standards ensure the financial statements from multiple companies are comparable. Because all entities follow the same rules, accounting standards make the financial statements credible and allow for more economic decisions based on accurate and consistent information.

Financial Accounting Standards Board (FASB)

An independent nonprofit organization, the Financial Accounting Standards Board (FASB) has the authority to establish and interpret accepted accounting principles (GAAP) in the United States for public and private companies and nonprofit organizations. GAAP refers to a set of standards for how companies, nonprofits, and governments should prepare and present their financial statements.

Why Are Accounting Standards Useful?

Accounting standards improve the transparency of financial reporting in all countries. They specify when and how economic events are to be recognized, measured, and displayed. External entities, such as banks, investors, and regulatory agencies, rely on accounting standards to ensure relevant and accurate information is provided about the entity. These technical pronouncements have ensured transparency in reporting and set the boundaries for financial reporting measures.

What Are Generally Accepted Accounting Principles (GAAP)?

In the United States, the Generally Accepted Accounting Principles (GAAP) form the set of accounting standards widely accepted for preparing financial statements. Its aim is to improve the clarity, consistency, and comparability of the communication of financial information. It is a common set of accounting principles, standards, and procedures issued by the Financial Accounting Standards Board (FASB). Public companies in the United States must follow GAAP when their accountants compile their financial statements.

What Are International Financial Reporting Standards (IFRS)?

International companies follow the International Financial Reporting Standards (IFRS), which are set by the International Accounting Standards Board and serve as the guideline for non-U.S. GAAP companies reporting financial statements. They were established to bring consistency to accounting standards and practices, regardless of the company or the country. IFRS is thought to be more dynamic than GAAP in that it is regularly being revised in response to an ever-changing financial environment.

Accounting Convention
What Is an Accounting Convention?

Accounting conventions are guidelines used to help companies determine how to record certain business transactions that have not yet been fully addressed by accounting standards. These procedures and principles are not legally binding but are accepted by accounting bodies. Basically, they are designed to promote consistency and help accountants overcome practical problems that can arise when preparing financial statements.

Key Takeaways

- Accounting conventions are guidelines used to help companies determine how to record business transactions not yet fully covered by accounting standards.

- They are accepted by accounting bodies but are not legally binding.

- If an oversight organization sets forth a guideline that addresses the same topic as the accounting convention, the accounting convention is no longer applicable.

- There are four widely recognized accounting conventions: conservatism, consistency, full disclosure, and materiality.

Understanding an Accounting Convention

Sometimes, there is not a definitive guideline in the accounting standards that govern a specific situation. In such cases, accounting conventions can be referred to.

Accounting is full of assumptions, concepts, standards, and conventions. Concepts such as relevance, reliability, materiality, and comparability are often supported by accounting conventions that help to standardize the financial reporting process.

In short, accounting conventions serve to fill in the gaps not yet addressed by accounting standards. If an oversight organization, such as the Securities and Exchange Commission (SEC) or the Financial Accounting Standards Board (FASB) sets forth a guideline that addresses the same topic as the accounting convention, the accounting convention is no longer applicable.

The scope and detail of accounting standards continue to widen, meaning that there are now fewer accounting conventions that can be used. Accounting conventions are not set in stone, either. Instead, they can evolve over time to reflect innovative ideas and opinions on the best way to record transactions.

Accounting conventions are important because they ensure that multiple different companies record transactions in the same way. Providing a standardized methodology makes it easier for investors to compare the financial results of different firms, such as competing ones operating in the same sector.

That said, accounting conventions are by no means flawless. They are sometimes loosely explained, presenting companies and their accountants with the opportunity to potentially bend or manipulate them to their advantage.

Accounting Convention Methods

There are four main accounting conventions designed to assist accountants:

- Conservatism: Playing it safe is both an accounting principle and convention. It tells accountants to err on the side of caution when providing estimates for assets and liabilities. That means that when two values of a transaction are available, the lower one should be favored. The general concept is to factor in the worst-case scenario of a firm's financial future.

- Consistency: A company should apply the same accounting principles across different accounting cycles. Once it chooses a method it is urged to stick with it in the future, unless it has a good reason to do otherwise. Without this convention, investors' ability to compare and assess how the company performs from one period to the next is made much more challenging.

- Full disclosure: Information considered potentially important and relevant must be revealed, regardless of whether it is detrimental to the company.

- Materiality: Like full disclosure, this convention urges companies to lay all their cards on the table. If an item or event is material, in other words important, it should be disclosed. The idea here is that any information that could influence the decision of a person looking at the financial statement must be included.

Areas Where Accounting Conventions Apply

Accounting conservatism may be applied to inventory valuation. When determining the reporting value of inventory, conservatism dictates that the lower of historical cost or replacement cost should be the monetary value.

Accounting conventions also dictate that adjustments to line items should not be made for inflation or market value. This means book value can sometimes be less than market value. For example, if a building costs $50,000 when it is purchased, it should remain on the books at $50,000, regardless of whether it is worth more now.

Estimations such as uncollectible accounts receivables and casualty losses also use the conservatism convention. If a company expects to win a litigation claim, it cannot report the gain until it meets all revenue recognition principles. However, if a litigation claim is expected to be lost, an estimated economic impact is required in the notes to the financial statements. Contingent liabilities such as royalty payments or unearned revenue are to be disclosed, too.

Accounting Policies
What Are Accounting Policies?

Accounting policies are the specific principles and procedures implemented by a company's management team that are used to prepare its financial statements. These include any accounting methods, measurement systems, and procedures for presenting disclosures. Accounting policies differ from accounting principles in that the principles are the accounting rules and the policies are a company's way of adhering to those rules.

Key Takeaways

- Accounting policies are procedures that a company uses to prepare financial statements. Unlike accounting principles, which are rules, accounting policies are the standards for following those rules.

- Accounting policies may be used to manipulate earnings legally.

- A company's choice in accounting policies will indicate whether management is aggressive or conservative in reporting its earnings.

- Accounting policies still need to adhere to accepted accounting principles (GAAP).

How Accounting Policies Are Used

Accounting policies are a set of standards that govern how a company prepares its financial statements. These policies are used to deal specifically with complicated accounting practices such as depreciation methods, recognition of goodwill, preparation of research and development (R&D) costs, inventory valuation, and the consolidation of financial accounts. These policies may differ from company to company, but all accounting policies are required to conform to generally accepted accounting principles (GAAP) and/or international financial reporting standards (IFRS).

Accounting principles can be thought of as a framework in which a company is expected to operate. However, the framework is flexible, and a company's management team can choose specific accounting policies that are advantageous to the financial reporting of the company. Because accounting principles are lenient at times, the specific policies of a company are especially important.

Looking into a company's accounting policies can signal whether management is conservative or aggressive when reporting earnings. This should be considered by investors when reviewing earnings reports to assess the quality of earnings. Also, external auditors who are hired to review a company's financial statements should review the company's policies to ensure they conform to GAAP.

Company management can select accounting policies that are advantageous to their own financial reporting, such as selecting a particular inventory valuation method.

Example of an Accounting Policy

Accounting policies can be used to legally manipulate earnings. For example, companies are allowed to value inventory using the average cost, first in first out (FIFO), or last in first out (LIFO) methods of accounting. Under the average cost method, when a company sells a product, the weighted average cost of all inventory produced or acquired in the accounting period is used to determine the cost of goods sold (COGS).

Under the FIFO inventory cost method, when a company sells a product, the cost of the inventory produced or acquired first is sold. Under the LIFO method, when a product is sold, the cost of the inventory produced last is sold. In periods of rising inventory prices, a company can use these accounting policies to increase or decrease its earnings.

For example, a company in the manufacturing industry buys inventory at $10 per unit for the first half of the month and $12 per unit for the second half of the month. The company ends up purchasing a total of 10 units at $10 and 10 units at $12 and sells a total of 15 units for the entire month.

If the company uses FIFO, its cost of goods sold is: (10 x $10) + (5 x $12) = $160. If it uses average cost, its cost of goods sold is: (15 x $11) = $165. If it uses LIFO, its cost of goods sold is: (10 x $12) + (5 x $10) = $170. It is therefore advantageous to use the FIFO method in periods of rising prices to minimize the cost of goods sold and increase earnings.

How Are Principles-Based and Rules-Based Accounting Different?

Nearly all companies are required to prepare their financial statements as set out by the Financial Accounting Standards Board (FASB), whose standards are generally principles-based. FASB uses these principles in establishing its accounting practices and methods. Law requires U.S. companies to adhere to accounting standards when reporting their financial statements, but the specifics can vary depending on where a company is headquartered.

Key Takeaways

- All companies are required to prepare their financial statements as set out by FASB, whose standards are generally principles-based.

- The rules based Generally Accepted Accounting Principles (GAAP) system is the accounting method used in the United States.

- Critics of principles-based accounting systems say they give companies too much freedom in reporting.

- On the other hand, critics of rules-based methods like GAAP cite that the system can often be too complex.

Understanding Principles-Based Accounting

Principles-based accounting is the most popular accounting method around the globe. Most countries opt for a principles-based system, as it is often better to adjust accounting principles to a company's transactions rather than adjusting a company's operations to accounting rules.

The international financial reporting standards (IFRS) system—the most common international accounting standard—is not a rules-based system. The IFRS states that a company's financial statements must be understandable, readable, comparable, and relevant to current financial transactions.

Rules-Based Accounting

Rules-based accounting is a standardized process of reporting financial statements. The Generally Accepted Accounting Principles (GAAP) system is the rules-based accounting method used in the United States. Companies and their accountants must adhere to the rules when they compile their financial statements. These allow investors an effortless way to compare the financial information of different companies.

There are 10 principles of the rules-based GAAP accounting system:

1. Regularity

2. Consistency

3. Sincerity with an accurate representation of the company's financial situation

4. Permanence of methods

5. No expectation of compensation

6. Prudence with no semblance of speculation

7. Continuity

8. Dividing entries across appropriate periods of time

9. Full disclosure in all financial reporting

10. Good faith and honesty in all transactions

The GAAP method is used when a company releases its financial statements to the public. It covers a number of things such as revenue recognition, balance sheet classification, and how outstanding shares are measured.

Companies and accountants that do not follow GAAP standards could be brought to court if their judgments and reporting of the financial statements were incorrect.

Principles-Based vs. Rules-Based Accounting

The fundamental advantage of principles-based accounting is that its broad guidelines can be practical for a variety of circumstances. Precise requirements can sometimes compel managers to manipulate the statements to fit what is compulsory.

On the other hand, when there are strict rules that need to be followed, like those in the U.S. GAAP system, the possibility of lawsuits is diminished. Having a set of rules can increase accuracy and reduce the ambiguity that can trigger aggressive reporting decisions by management.

Compliance to GAAP helps to ensure transparency in the financial reporting process by standardizing the various methods, terminology, definitions, and financial ratios. For example, GAAP allows investors to compare the financial statements of two companies by having standardized reporting methods. Companies must formulate their balance sheet, income statement, and cash flow statement in the same manner, so that they can be more easily evaluated.

If companies were able to report their financial numbers in any manner they chose, investors would be open to risk. Without a rules-based accounting system, companies could report only the numbers that made them appear financially successful while avoiding reporting any negative news or losses.

Problems With Both Systems

The main problem overall is that there is no one set accounting method that has been universally adopted. There are currently more than 144 jurisdictions that use IFRS as their accounting standards, while the U.S. uses the rules-based GAAP method.5 As a result, investments, acquisitions, and mergers may require a different lens when comparing international competitors such as Exxon and BP, which use different accounting methods.

Critics of principles-based accounting systems say they can give companies far too much freedom and do not prescribe transparency. They believe because companies do not have to follow specific rules that have been set out, their reporting may provide an inaccurate picture of its financial health.

In the case of rules-based methods like GAAP, complex rules can cause unnecessary complications in the preparation of financial statements. And having strict rules means that accountants may try to make their companies more profitable than they are because of the responsibility to their shareholders.

Example of Accounting Manipulation

Enron was a major energy company in the 1990s. In 2001, Enron shareholders lost $75 billion in value after the company's executives used fraudulent accounting practices to overstate revenue while hiding debt in its subsidiaries.

Enron declared bankruptcy–and with $63 billion in assets–was the largest U.S. bankruptcy at that time. The company's collapse sent shockwaves throughout the financial markets leading to a wave of additional regulations.

When contemplating which accounting method is best, make certain that the information provided in the financial statements is relevant, reliable, and comparable across reporting periods and entities. Although there are benefits to principle-based accounting, it is recognized that the method may need to be modified to make it more effective and efficient.

Accounting Method
What Is an Accounting Method?

An accounting method refers to the rules a company follows in reporting revenues and expenses. The two primary methods of accounting are accrual accounting (used by companies) and cash accounting (used by individuals).

Cash accounting reports revenues and expenses as they are received and paid through cash inflows and outflows; accrual accounting reports them as they are earned and incurred through sales and purchases on credit and by using accounts receivable & accounts payable. Accepted accounting principles (GAAP) requires accrual accounting.

Key Takeaways

- An accounting method consists of the rules and procedures a company follows in reporting its revenues and expenses.

- The two main accounting methods are cash accounting and accrual accounting.

- Cash accounting records revenues and expenses when they are received and paid.

- Accrual accounting records revenues and expenses when they occur. Accepted accounting principles (GAAP) requires accrual accounting.

- The Internal Revenue Services (IRS) requires accrual accounting for businesses making an average of $25 million or more in sales for the preceding three years.

- Once a company chooses an accounting method, it must stick to that method per rules set by the

IRS and requires approval if it wants to change its accounting method.

Understanding an Accounting Method

All businesses need to keep accounting records. Public companies are required to do so. Accounting allows a business to monitor every aspect of its finances, from revenues to costs to taxes and more. Without accurate accounting, a business would not know where it stood financially, resulting in its demise.

Accounting is also needed to pay accurate taxes to the Internal Revenue Service (IRS). If the IRS ever conducts an audit on a company, it looks at a company's accounting records and methods. Furthermore, the IRS requires taxpayers to choose an accounting method that accurately reflects their income and to be consistent in their choice of accounting method from year to year.

This is because switching between methods would potentially allow a company to manipulate revenue to minimize their tax burdens. As such, IRS approval is required to change methods. Companies may use a hybrid of the two methods, which is allowable under IRS rules if specified requirements are met.

Types of Accounting Methods

Cash Accounting

Cash accounting is an accounting method that is simple and is commonly used by small businesses. In cash accounting, transactions are only recorded when cash is spent or received.

In cash accounting, a sale is recorded when the payment is received, and an expense is recorded only when a bill is paid. The cash accounting method is, of course, the method most people use in managing their personal finances and it is appropriate for businesses up to a certain size.

If a business generates more than $25 million in average annual gross receipts for the preceding three years, however, it must use the accrual method, according to Internal Revenue Service rules.

Accrual Accounting

Accrual accounting is based on the matching principle, which is intended to match the timing of revenue and expense recognition. By matching revenues with expenses, the accrual method gives a more accurate picture of a company's true financial condition.

Under the accrual method, transactions are recorded when they are incurred rather than awaiting payment. This means a purchase order is recorded as revenue even though the funds are not received immediately. The same goes for expenses in that they are recorded even though no payment has been made.

Example of an Accounting Method

The value of accrual accounting becomes more evident for large, complex businesses. A construction company, for example, may undertake a long-term project and may not receive complete cash payments until the project is complete.

Under cash accounting rules, the company would incur many expenses but would not recognize revenue until cash was received from the customer. So, the accounting book of the company would look weak until the revenue came in. If this company was looking for debt financing from a bank, for example, the cash accounting method makes it look like a poor bet because it is incurring expenses but no revenue.

Under accrual accounting, the construction company would recognize a percentage of revenue and expenses corresponding to the portion of the project that was complete. This is known as the percentage of completion method. How much actual cash coming into the company, however, would be evident in the cash flow statement. This method would show a prospective lender a much completer and more accurate picture of the company's revenue pipeline.

Accrual Accounting
What Is Accrual Accounting?

Accrual accounting is one of two accounting methods; the other is cash accounting. Accrual accounting measures a company's performance and position by recognizing economic events regardless of when cash transactions occur, whereas cash accounting only records transactions when payment occurs.

Key Takeaways:

- Accrual accounting is an accounting method where revenue or expenses are recorded when a transaction occurs rather than when payment is received or made.

- The method follows the matching principle, which says that revenues and expenses should be recognized in the same period.

- Cash accounting is the other accounting method, which recognizes transactions only when payment is exchanged.

How To Decipher Accrual Accounting

How Accrual Accounting Works

The general concept of accrual accounting is that economic events are recognized by matching revenues to expenses (the matching principle) at the time when the transaction occurs rather than when payment is made or received. This method allows the current cash inflows or outflows to be combined with future expected cash inflows or outflows to give a more accurate picture of a company's current financial position.

Accrual accounting is considered the standard accounting practice for most companies except for exceedingly small businesses and individuals. The Internal Revenue Service (IRS) allows qualifying small businesses (less than $25 million in annual revenues) to choose their preferred method.1 The accrual method does provide a more accurate picture of the company's current condition, but its relative complexity makes it more expensive to implement.

This method arose from the increasing complexity of business transactions and a desire for more accurate financial information. Selling on credit, and projects that provide revenue streams over a long period, affect a company's financial condition at the time of a transaction. Therefore, it makes sense that such events should also be reflected in the financial statements during the same reporting period that these transactions occur.

Under accrual accounting, firms have immediate feedback on their expected cash inflows and outflows, which makes it easier for businesses to manage their current resources and plan.

Accrual accounting provides a more accurate picture of a company's financial position some small businesses use cash accounting.

Accrual Accounting vs. Cash Accounting

Accrual accounting can be contrasted with cash accounting, which recognizes transactions only when there is an exchange of cash. Accrual accounting is always required for companies that carry inventory or make sales on credit.

For example, consider a consulting company that provides a $5,000 service to a client on Oct. 30. The client receives the bill for services rendered and makes a cash payment on Nov. 25. The entry of this transaction will be recorded differently under the cash and accrual methods. The revenue generated by the consulting services will only be recognized under the cash method when the company receives payment. A company that uses the cash accounting method will record $5,000 revenue on Nov. 25.

Accrual accounting, however, says that the cash method is not accurate because it is likely, if not certain, that the company will receive the cash at some point in the future because the services have been provided. The accrual method recognizes the revenue when the clients' services are concluded even though the cash payment is not yet in the bank. Revenue will be recognized as earned on Oct. 30. The sale is booked to an account known as accounts receivable, found in the current assets section of the balance sheet.

A company that incurs an expense that it has yet to pay for will recognize the business expense on the day the expense arises. Under the accrual method of accounting, the company receiving goods or services on credit must report the liability no later than the date the goods were received. The accrued expense will be recorded as an account payable under the current liabilities section of the balance sheet and also as an expense in the income statement. On the general ledger, when the bill is paid, the accounts payable account is debited, and the cash account is credited.

What Are the Types of Accrual Accounts?

There are several types of accrual accounts. The most common include accounts payable, accounts receivable, goodwill, accrued interest earned, and accrued tax liabilities.

Accounts payable refers to debts a company incurs when it receives goods or services from its vendors before it has actually paid for them. Using the accrual accounting method, when a company incurs an expense, the debt is recorded on the balance sheet as an accounts payable liability and on the income statement as an expense.

What Is an Example of Accrual Accounting?

Suppose an appliance store sells a refrigerator to a customer on credit. Depending on the terms of its agreement with its customers, it may take many months or years before the store receives payment in full from the customer for the refrigerator. Using the accrual accounting method, the store will record the accrued revenue from the sale when the refrigerator leaves the store, not at some date in the future.

Does the IRS Require Accrual Accounting for Companies?

While the IRS does not require a single method of accounting for all businesses, it does impose certain limitations that impact which accounting method a company can use. For example, a company cannot use the cash method if it is a corporation (other than an S corporation) with average annual gross receipts greater than $25 million for the prior three tax years. In these situations, the IRS requires the corporation to change to an accrual accounting method.2

What Is Modified Accrual Accounting?

Modified accrual accounting is an alternative accounting method that combines elements from accrual accounting with cash basis accounting. Because modified accrual accounting does not comply with accepted accounting principles (GAAP), public companies do not use it. However, the accounting method is widely accepted and used by government agencies.

Cash Accounting
What Is Cash Accounting?

Cash accounting is an accounting method where payment receipts are recorded during the period in which they are received, and expenses are recorded in the period in which they are actually paid. In other words, revenues and expenses are recorded when cash is received and paid, respectively.

Cash accounting is also called cash-basis accounting; and may be contrasted with accrual accounting, which recognizes income at the time the revenue is earned and records expenses when liabilities are incurred regardless of when cash is actually received or paid.

Key Takeaways

- Cash accounting is simple and straightforward. Transactions are recorded only when money goes in or out of an account.

- Cash accounting does not work as well for larger companies or companies with a large inventory because it can obscure the true financial position.

- The alternative to cash accounting is accrual accounting, where transactions are recorded as revenues are earned and expenses are incurred, regardless of the exchange of cash.

Understanding Cash Accounting

Cash accounting is one of two forms of accounting. The other is accrual accounting, where revenue and expenses are recorded when they are incurred. Small businesses often use cash accounting because it is simpler and more straightforward, and it provides a clear picture of how much money the business has on hand. Corporations, however, are required to use accrual accounting under Generally Accepted Accounting Principles (GAAP).

When transactions are recorded on a cash basis, they affect a company's books with a delay from when a transaction is consummated. As a result, cash accounting is often less accurate than accrual accounting in the short term.

Most small businesses are permitted to choose between either the cash and accrual method of accounting, but the IRS requires businesses with over $25 million in annual gross receipts to use the accrual method. In addition, the Tax Reform Act of 1986 prohibits the cash accounting method from being used for C corporations, tax shelters, certain types of trusts, and partnerships that have C Corporation partners.2 Note that companies must use the same accounting method for tax reporting as they do for their own internal bookkeeping.

Example of Cash Accounting

Under the cash accounting method, say Company A receives $10,000 from the sale of 10 computers sold to Company B on November 2, and records the sale as having occurred on November 2. The fact that Company B in fact placed the order for the computers back on October 5 is deemed irrelevant, because it did not pay for them until they were physically delivered on November 2.

Under accrual accounting, by contrast, Company A would have recorded the $10,000 sale on October 5, even though no cash had yet changed hands.

Similarly, under cash accounting companies record expenses when they pay them, not when they incur them. If Company C hires Company D for pest control on January 15, but does not pay the invoice for the service completed until February 15, the expense would not be recognized until February 15 under cash accounting. Under accrual accounting, however, the expense would be recorded in the books on January 15 when it was initiated.

Limitations of Cash Accounting

A main drawback of cash accounting is that it may not provide an accurate picture of the liabilities that have been incurred (i.e. accrued) but not yet paid for, so that the business might appear to be better off than it really is. On the other hand, cash accounting also means that a business that has just completed a large job for which it is awaiting payment may appear to be less successful than it really is because it has expended the materials and labor for the job but not yet collected payment. Therefore, cash accounting can both overstate or understate the condition of the business if collections or payments happen to be particularly high or low in one period versus another.

There are also some potentially negative tax consequences for businesses that adopt the cash accounting method. In general, businesses can only deduct expenses that are recognized within the current tax year.3 If a company incurs expenses in December 2019, but does not make payments against the expenses until January 2020, it would not be able to claim a deduction for the fiscal year ended 2019, which could significantly affect the business' bottom line. Likewise, a company that receives payment from a client in 2020 for services rendered in 2019 will only be allowed to include the revenue in its financial statements for 2020.

Accrual Accounting vs. Cash Basis Accounting: What's the Difference?

Accrual Accounting vs. Cash Basis Accounting: An Overview

The main difference between accrual and cash basis accounting lies in the timing of when revenue and expenses are recognized. The cash method is a more immediate recognition of revenue and expenses, while the accrual method focuses on anticipated revenue and expenses.

Key Takeaways

- Accrual accounting means revenue and expenses are recognized and recorded when they occur, while cash basis accounting means these line items are not documented until cash exchanges hands.

- Cash basis accounting is easier, but accrual accounting portrays a more accurate portrait of a company's health by including accounts payable and accounts receivable.

- The accrual method is the most used method, especially by publicly traded companies as it smooths out earnings over time.

Accrual Accounting Method

Revenue is accounted for when it is earned. Typically, revenue is recorded before any money changes hands. Unlike the cash method, the accrual method records revenue when a product or service is delivered to a customer with the expectation that money will be paid in the future. Expenses of goods and services are recorded despite no cash being paid out yet for those expenses.

Cash Basis Accounting

Revenue is reported on the income statement only when cash is received. Expenses are only recorded when cash is paid out. The cash method is mostly used by small businesses and for personal finances.

Key Differences

The key advantage of the cash method is its simplicity—it only accounts for cash paid or received. Tracking the cash flow of a company is also easier with the cash method.

But a disadvantage of the cash method is that it might overstate the health of a company that is cash-rich but has large sums of accounts payables that far exceed the cash on the books and the company's current revenue stream. An investor might conclude the company is making a profit when the company is losing money.

Meanwhile, the advantage of the accrual method is that it includes accounts receivables and payables and, as a result, is a more accurate picture of the profitability of a company, particularly in the long term. The reason for this is that the accrual method records all revenues when they are earned and all expenses when they are incurred.

For example, a company might have sales in the current quarter that would not be recorded under the cash method because revenue is not expected until the following quarter. An investor might conclude the company is unprofitable when the company is doing well.

The disadvantage of the accrual method is that it does not track cash flow and, as a result, might not account for a company with a major cash shortage in the short term, despite looking profitable in the long term. Another disadvantage of the accrual method is that it can be more complicated to implement since it's necessary to account for items like unearned revenue and prepaid expenses.

Special Considerations

The accrual method is most used by companies, particularly publicly traded companies. One reason for the accrual method's popularity is that it smooths out earnings over time since it accounts for all revenues and expenses as they are generated instead of being recorded intermittently under the cash-basis method. For example, under the cash method, retailers would look extremely profitable in Q4 as consumers buy for the holiday season but would look unprofitable in Q1 as consumer spending declines following the holiday rush.

Both methods have their advantages and disadvantages, and each only shows part of the financial health of a company. Understanding both the accrual method and a company's cash flow with the cash method is important when making an investment decision.

Accrual Accounting vs. Cash Basis Accounting Example

Let us say you own a business that sells machinery. If you sell $5,000 worth of machinery, under the cash method, that amount is not recorded in the books until the customer hands you the money or you receive the check. Under the accrual method, the $5,000 is recorded as revenue immediately when the sale is made, even if you receive the money a few days or weeks later.

The same principle applies to expenses. If you receive an electric bill for $1,700, under the cash method, the amount is not added to the books until you pay the bill. However, under the accrual method, the $1,700 is recorded as an expense the day you receive the bill.

Financial Accounting Standards Board (FASB)
What Is the Financial Accounting Standards Board (FASB)?

The Financial Accounting Standards Board (FASB) is an independent nonprofit organization responsible for establishing accounting and financial reporting standards for companies and nonprofit organizations in the United States, following generally accepted accounting principles (GAAP). The FASB was formed in

1973 to succeed the Accounting Principles Board and carry on its mission. It is based in Norwalk, Conn.

Key Takeaways:

- The Financial Accounting Standards Board (FASB) sets accounting rules for public and private companies and nonprofits in the United States.

- A related organization, the Governmental Accounting Standards Board (GASB), sets rules for state and local governments.

- In recent years, the FASB has been working with the International Accounting Standards Board (IASB) to establish compatible standards worldwide.

How the Financial Accounting Standards Board (FASB) Works

The Financial Accounting Standards Board has the authority to establish and interpret generally accepted accounting principles (GAAP) in the United States for public and private companies and nonprofit organizations. GAAP is a set of standards that companies, nonprofits, and governments should follow when preparing and presenting their financial statements, including any related party transactions.

The Securities and Exchange Commission (SEC) recognizes the FASB as the accounting standard setter for public companies. It is also recognized by state accounting boards, the American Institute of Certified Public Accountants (AICPA), and other organizations in the field.

The Financial Accounting Standards Board is part of a larger, independent nonprofit group that also includes the Financial Accounting Foundation (FAF), the Financial Accounting Standards Advisory Council (FASAC), the Governmental Accounting Standards Board (GASB), and the Governmental Accounting Standards Advisory Council (GASAC).

The GASB, which is similar in function to the FASB, was established in 1984 to set accounting and financial reporting standards for state and local governments across the United States. The FAF oversees both the FASB and the GASB. The two advisory councils provide guidance in their respective areas.

Collectively, the organizations' mission is to improve financial accounting and reporting standards so that the information is useful to investors and other users of financial reports. The organizations also educate stakeholders on how to understand and implement the standards most effectively.

The FASB is governed by seven full-time board members, who are required to sever their ties to the companies or organizations they work for before joining the board. Board members are appointed by the FAF's board of trustees for five-year terms and may serve for up to 10 years.

In 2009, the FAF launched the FASB Accounting Standards Codification, an online research tool designed as a sole source for authoritative, nongovernmental, generally accepted accounting principles in the United States. According to the FAF, the tool "reorganizes the thousands of U.S. GAAP pronouncements into roughly 90 accounting topics and displays all topics using a consistent structure." The website also provides relevant Securities and Exchange Commission (SEC) guidance on those topics. A "basic view" version is free, while the more comprehensive "professional view" is available by paid subscription.

FASB vs. IASB

The London-based International Accounting Standards Board (IASB), founded in 2001 to replace an older standards organization, is responsible for the International Financial Reporting Standards (IFRS), which are now used in many countries throughout the world. In recent years, the FASB has been working with the IASB on an initiative to improve financial reporting and the comparability of financial reports globally.

Generally Accepted Accounting Principles (GAAP)

What Are Generally Accepted Accounting Principles (GAAP)?

Generally accepted accounting principles (GAAP) refer to a common set of accounting principles, standards, and procedures issued by the Financial Accounting Standards Board (FASB). Public companies in the U.S. must follow GAAP when their accountants compile their financial statements.

Key Takeaways

- GAAP is the set of accounting principles set forth by the FASB that U.S. companies must follow when putting together financial statements.

- GAAP aims to improve the clarity, consistency, and comparability of the communication of financial information.

- GAAP may be contrasted with pro forma accounting, which is a non-GAAP financial reporting method.

- The goal of GAAP is to ensure a company's financial statements are complete, consistent, and comparable.

- There are 10 key concepts that guide the principles of GAAP.

GAAP

Understanding GAAP

GAAP is a combination of authoritative standards (set by policy boards) and the commonly accepted ways of recording and reporting accounting information. GAAP aims to improve the clarity, consistency, and comparability of the communication of financial information.

GAAP may be contrasted with pro forma accounting, which is a non-GAAP financial reporting method. Internationally, the equivalent to GAAP in the U.S. is referred to as International Financial Reporting Standards (IFRS). IFRS is currently used in 166 jurisdictions.

GAAP helps govern the world of accounting according to general rules and guidelines. It attempts to standardize and regulate the definitions, assumptions, and methods used in accounting across all industries. GAAP covers such topics as revenue recognition, balance sheet classification, and materiality.

The ultimate goal of GAAP is to ensure a company's financial statements are complete, consistent, and comparable. This makes it easier for investors to analyze and extract useful information from the company's financial statements, including trend data over a period. It also facilitates the comparison of financial information across different companies.

10 Principles of GAAP

There are 10 general concepts that lay out the main mission of GAAP.

1. Principle of Regularity

The accountant has adhered to GAAP rules and regulations as a standard.

2. Principle of Consistency

Accountants commit to applying the same standards throughout the reporting process, from one period to the next, to ensure financial comparability between periods. Accountants are expected to fully disclose and explain the reasons behind any changed or updated standards in the footnotes to the financial statements.

3. Principle of Sincerity

The accountant strives to provide an accurate and impartial depiction of a company's financial situation.

4. Principle of Permanence of Methods

The procedures used in financial reporting should be consistent, allowing a comparison of the company's financial information.

5. Principle of Non-Compensation

Both negatives and positives should be reported with full transparency and without the expectation of debt compensation.

6. Principle of Prudence

This refers to emphasizing fact-based financial data representation that is not clouded by speculation.

7. Principle of Continuity

While valuing assets, it should be assumed the business will continue to operate.

8. Principle of Periodicity

Entries should be distributed across the appropriate periods of time. For example, revenue should be reported in its relevant accounting period.

9. Principle of Materiality

Accountants must strive to fully disclose all financial data and accounting information in financial reports.

10. Principle of Utmost Good Faith

Derived from the Latin phrase uberrimae fidei used within the insurance industry. It presupposes that parties remain honest in all transactions.

Compliance With GAAP

If a corporation's stock is publicly traded, its financial statements must adhere to rules established by the U.S. Securities and Exchange Commission (SEC). The SEC requires that publicly traded companies in the U.S. regularly file GAAP-compliant financial statements in order to remain publicly listed on the stock exchanges.3 GAAP compliance is ensured through an appropriate auditor's opinion, resulting from an external audit by a certified public accounting (CPA) firm.

Although it is not required for non-publicly traded companies, GAAP is viewed favorably by lenders and creditors. Most financial institutions will require annual GAAP-compliant financial statements as a part of their debt covenants when issuing business loans. As a result, most companies in the United States do follow GAAP.

If a financial statement is not prepared using GAAP, investors should be cautious. Without GAAP, comparing financial statements of different companies would be extremely difficult, even within the same industry, making an apples-to-apples comparison hard. Some companies may report both GAAP and non-GAAP measures when reporting their financial results. GAAP regulations require that non-GAAP measures be identified in financial statements and other public disclosures, such as press releases.

The hierarchy of GAAP is designed to improve financial reporting. It consists of a framework for selecting the principles that public accountants should use in preparing financial statements in line with U.S. GAAP. The hierarchy is broken down as follows:

- Statements by the Financial Accounting Standards Board (FASB) and Accounting Research Bulletins and Accounting Principles Board opinions by the American Institute of Certified Public Accountants (AICPA)

- FASB Technical Bulletins and AICPA Industry Audit and Accounting Guides and Statements of Position

- AICPA Accounting Standards Executive Committee Practice Bulletins, positions of the FASB Emerging Issues Task Force (EITF), and topics discussed in Appendix D of EITF Abstracts

- FASB implementation guides, AICPA Accounting Interpretations, AICPA Industry Audit, and Accounting Guides, Statements of Position not cleared by the FASB, and accounting practices that are widely accepted and followed

Accountants are directed to first consult sources at the top of the hierarchy and then proceed to lower levels only if there is no relevant pronouncement at a higher level. The FASB's Statement of Financial Accounting Standards No. 162 provides a detailed explanation of the hierarchy.4

GAAP vs. IFRS

GAAP is focused on the accounting and financial reporting of U.S. companies. The Financial Accounting Standards Board (FASB), an independent nonprofit organization, is responsible for establishing these accounting and financial reporting standards. The international alternative to GAAP is the International Financial Reporting Standards (IFRS), set by the International Accounting Standards Board (IASB).

The IASB and the FASB have been working on the convergence of IFRS and GAAP since 2002. Due to the progress achieved in this partnership, the SEC, in 2007, removed the requirement for non-U.S. companies registered in America to reconcile their financial reports with GAAP if their accounts already complied with IFRS. This was a big achievement because prior to the ruling, non-U.S. companies trading on U.S.

exchanges had to provide GAAP-compliant financial statements.

Some differences that still exist between both accounting rules include:

- LIFO Inventory: While GAAP allows companies to use the Last In First Out (LIFO) as an inventory cost method, it is prohibited under IFRS.

- Research and Development Costs: These costs are to be charged to expense as they are incurred under GAAP. Under IFRS, the costs can be capitalized and amortized over multiple periods if certain conditions are met.

- Reversing Write-Downs: GAAP specifies that the amount of write-down of an inventory or fixed asset cannot be reversed if the market value of the asset subsequently increases. The write-down can be reversed under IFRS.

As corporations increasingly need to navigate global markets and conduct operations worldwide, international standards are becoming increasingly popular at the expense of GAAP, even in the U.S. All S&P 500 companies report at least one non-GAAP measure of earnings as of 2019.

Special Considerations

GAAP is only a set of standards. Although these principles work to improve the transparency in financial statements, they do not provide any guarantee that a company's financial statements are free from errors or omissions that are intended to mislead investors. There is plenty of room within GAAP for unscrupulous accountants to distort figures. So even when a company uses GAAP, you still need to scrutinize its financial statements.

Where Are Generally Accepted Accounting Principles (GAAP) Used?

GAAP is a set of procedures and guidelines used by companies to prepare their financial statements and other accounting disclosures. The standards are prepared by the Financial Accounting Standards Board (FASB), which is an independent non-profit organization. The purpose of GAAP standards is to help ensure that the financial information provided to investors and regulators is accurate, dependable, and consistent with one another.

Why Is GAAP Important?

GAAP is important because it helps maintain trust in the financial markets. If not for GAAP, investors would be more reluctant to trust the information presented to them by companies because they would have less confidence in its integrity. Without that trust, we might see fewer transactions, potentially leading to higher transaction costs and a less robust economy. GAAP also helps investors analyze companies by making it easier to perform "apples to apples" comparisons between one company and another.

What Are Non-GAAP Measures?

Companies are still allowed to present certain figures without abiding by GAAP guidelines, if they clearly identify those figures as not conforming to GAAP. Companies sometimes do so when they believe that the GAAP rules are not flexible enough to capture certain nuances about their operations. In that situation, they might provide specially designed non-GAAP metrics, in addition to the other disclosures required under GAAP. Investors should be skeptical about non-GAAP measures, however, as they can sometimes be used in a misleading manner.

International Financial Reporting Standards (IFRS)
What Are International Financial Reporting Standards (IFRS)?

International Financial Reporting Standards (IFRS) are a set of accounting rules for the financial statements of public companies that are intended to make them consistent, transparent, and easily comparable around the world.

IFRS have been adopted for use in 120 nations, including those in the European Union. The United States uses a different system, the Generally Accepted Accounting Principles (GAAP).

The IFRS are issued by the International Accounting Standards Board (IASB).

IFRS are sometimes confused with International Accounting Standards (IAS), which are the older standards that IFRS replaced in 2001.

Key Takeaways

- International Financial Reporting Standards (IFRS) were created to bring consistency and integrity to accounting standards and practices, regardless of the company or the country.

- They were issued by the London-based Accounting Standards Board (IASB) and address record keeping, account reporting, and other aspects of financial reporting.

- IFRS fosters greater corporate transparency.

International Financial Reporting Standards (IFRS)

Understanding IFRS

IFRS specify in detail how companies must maintain their records and report their expenses and income. They were established to create a common accounting language that could be understood globally by investors, auditors, government regulators, and other interested parties.

The standards are designed to bring consistency to accounting language, practices, and statements, and to help businesses and investors make educated financial analyses and decisions.

They were developed by the International Accounting Standards Board, which is part of the not-for-profit, London-based IFRS Foundation. The Foundation says it sets the standards to "bring transparency, accountability, and efficiency to financial markets around the world."

IFRS vs. GAAP

Public companies in the U.S. are required to use a rival system, the Generally Accepted Accounting Principles (GAAP). The GAAP standards were developed by the Financial Standards Accounting Board (FSAB) and the Governmental Accounting Standards Board (GASB).

The Securities and Exchange Commission (SEC) has said it will not switch to International Financial Reporting Standards but will continue reviewing a proposal to allow IFRS information to supplement U.S. financial filings.

There are differences between IFRS and GAAP reporting. For example, IFRS is not as strict in defining revenue and allows companies to report revenue sooner. A balance sheet using this system might show a higher stream of revenue than a GAAP version of the same balance sheet.

IFRS also has different requirements for reporting expenses. For example, if a company is spending money on development or on investment for the future, it does not necessarily have to be reported as an expense. It can be capitalized instead.

Standard IFRS Requirements

IFRS covers a wide range of accounting activities. There are certain aspects of business practice for which IFRS set mandatory rules.

- Statement of Financial Position: This is the balance sheet. IFRS influences the ways in which the components of a balance sheet are reported.

- Statement of Comprehensive Income: This can take the form of one statement or be separated into a profit and loss statement and a statement of other income, including property and equipment.

- Statement of Changes in Equity: Also known as a statement of retained earnings, this documents the company's change in earnings or profit for the given financial period.

- Statement of Cash Flows: This report summarizes the company's financial transactions in the given period, separating cash flow into operations, investing, and financing.

In addition to these basic reports, a company must give a summary of its accounting policies. The full report is often seen side by side with the previous report to show the changes in profit and loss.

A parent company must create separate account reports for each of its subsidiary companies.

Chinese companies do not use IFRS or GAAP. They use Chinese Accounting Standards for Business Enterprises (ASBEs).

History of IFRS

IFRS originated in the European Union with the intention of making business affairs and accounts accessible across the continent. It was quickly adopted as a common accounting language.

Although the U.S. and some other countries do not use IFRS, 120 countries do, making IFRS the most used set of standards globally.

Who Uses IFRS?

IFRS are required to be used by public companies based in a total of 120 countries, including all the nations in the European Union as well as Canada, India, Russia, South Korea, South Africa, and Chile.

The U.S. and China each have their own systems.

Only a few countries have publicly traded companies but require neither system. They include Egypt, Bolivia, Guinea-Bissau, Macao, and Niger.

How Does IFRS Differ from GAAP?

The two systems have the same goal: clarity and honesty in financial reporting by publicly traded companies.

IFRS was designed as is a standards-based approach that could be used internationally. GAAP is a rules-based system used primarily in the U.S.

Although most of the world uses IFRS standards, it is still not part of the U.S. financial accounting world. The SEC continues to review switching to the IFRS but has yet to do so.

Several methodological differences exist between the two systems. For instance, GAAP allows a company to use either of two inventory cost methods: First in, First out (FIFO) or Last in, First out (LIFO). LIFO, however, is banned under IFRS.

Why Is IFRS Important?

IFRS fosters transparency and trust in the global financial markets and the companies that list their shares on them. If such standards did not exist, investors would be more reluctant to believe the financial statements and other information presented to them by companies. Without that trust, we might see fewer transactions and a less robust economy.

IFRS also helps investors analyze companies by making it easier to perform "apples to apples" comparisons between one company and another and for fundamental analysis of a company's performance.

IFRS vs. GAAP: What's the Difference?
IFRS vs. GAAP: An Overview

Systems of accounting, or accounting standards, are guidelines and regulations issued by governing bodies. They dictate how a company records its finances, how it presents its financial statements, and how it accounts for things such as inventories, depreciation, and amortization.

How a company reports these figures will have a significant impact on the figures that appear in financial statements and regulatory filings. Investors and financial analysts must be sure they understand which set of standards a company is using, and how its bottom line or financial ratios will change if the accounting system were different. To answer this question, it's important to differentiate between International Financial Reporting Standards (IFRS) and Generally Accepted Accounting Principles (GAAP) to get a better grasp of the function they serve in the world of accounting.

Key Takeaways

- Accounting standards and guidelines for best practices differ by region and may be company specific.

- IFRS is a global set of standards used by 15 of the G20 countries.1

- GAAP is specific to the United States and has been adopted by the SEC.2

IFRS

IFRS stands for International Financial Reporting Standards. The International Accounting Standards Board (IASB) is the accounting standards body for the IFRS Foundation.3

The predecessor to the IFRS Foundation, the International Accounting Standards Committee, was formed in 1973. Initial members were accounting bodies from Australia, Canada, France, Germany, Japan, Mexico, Netherlands, the U.K., and the United States.4 Today, IFRS has become the global standard for the preparation of public company financial statements and 144 out of 166 jurisdictions require IFRS standards.

Fifteen of the G20 countries have adopted IFRS. China, India, and Indonesia have national accounting standards that are like IFRS, while Japan allows companies to follow the standards voluntarily. In the United States, foreign listed companies may use IFRS and are no longer required to reconcile their financial statements with GAAP.

The IFRS Foundation works with more than a dozen consultative bodies, representing the many different stakeholder groups that are impacted by financial reporting.

GAAP

GAAP stands for generally accepted accounting principles and is the standard adopted by the Securities and Exchange Commission (SEC) in the U.S.2 Except for foreign companies, all companies that are publicly traded must adhere to the GAAP system of accounting.6

The best way to think of GAAP is as a set of rules that companies follow when their accountants report their financial statements. These rules help investors analyze and find the information they need to make sound financial decisions.

Key Differences

IFRS is a principle of the standard-based approach and is used internationally, while GAAP is a rule-based system compiled in the U.S.

The IASB does not set GAAP, nor does it have any legal authority over GAAP. The IASB can be thought of as a very influential group of people who engage in debating and making up accounting rules. However, a lot of people do listen to what the IASB has to say on matters of accounting.

When the IASB sets a brand new accounting standard, several countries tend to adopt the standard, or at least interpret it, and fit it into their individual country's accounting standards. These standards, as set by each country's accounting standards board, will in turn influence what becomes GAAP for each country. For example, in the United States, the Financial Accounting Standards Board (FASB) makes up the rules and regulations which become GAAP.

Although most of the world uses IFRS standards, it is not part of the financial world in the U.S. The SEC continues to review switching to the IFRS but has yet to do so.

Special Considerations

Some major differences exist between the two sets of accounting standards. These include:

- Inventory: The first is with the LIFO Inventory. GAAP allows companies to use the Last in, First out (LIFO) as an inventory cost method. But LIFO is banned under IFRS.

- Development costs: Under GAAP, these costs are considered expenses. Under IFRS, the costs are capitalized and amortized over multiple periods. This applies to the internal costs of developing any intangible assets.

- Write-downs: GAAP specifies the write-down amount of an inventory or fixed asset cannot be reversed if the market value of the asset subsequently increases. On the other hand, the IFRS allows the write-down to be reversed. This results in inventory values fluctuating more frequently under IFRS than under GAAP.

- Fixed Assets: Under GAAP, fixed assets such as property, plant, and equipment (PP&E), must be recorded at historical cost (the purchase price), and depreciated accordingly. Under IFRS, fixed assets are also valued at cost, but companies are allowed to revalue fixed assets to the fair market value.

How Does US Accounting Differ From International Accounting?

Despite major efforts by the Financial Accounting Standards Board (FASB) and the International Accounting Standards Board (IASB), significant differences remain between accounting practices in the United States and the rest of the world. For example, U.S. companies are allowed to use last in, first out (LIFO) as an inventory-costing method. However, LIFO is banned under a competing set of accounting standards used in much of the world.

International practices are compiled in the International Financial Reporting Standards (IFRS), as set forth by the IASB. In the U.S, the FASB releases statements of financial accounting that, when combined, form generally accepted accounting principles (GAAP).

According to the American Institute of Certified Public Accountants, the greatest difference between the IFRS and GAAP is "that IFRS provides much less overall detail." Other significant differences include how comparative financial information is presented, how the balance sheet and income statements are laid out, and how debts are treated.

Inventory Accounting Differences

GAAP allows LIFO carrying cost of inventory accounting, while the IFRS explicitly prohibits any company from using LIFO. Instead, international standards dictate that the same cost formula must be applied to all inventories of a similar nature.

Under GAAP, inventory is carried at the lower of cost or market, with the market being defined as current replacement cost, with some exceptions. Inventory under IFRS is carried at the lower of cost or net realizable value, which is the estimated selling price minus costs of completion and other costs necessary to make a sale.

Other inventory differences include how markdowns are allowed under the retail inventory method or RIM, and how inventory write-downs are reversed.

Long-Lived Assets

GAAP does not allow for assets to be revalued; IFRS allows for some revaluation based on fair value, as long as it is completed regularly. The depreciation of the components of long-lived assets is very uncommon, though technically allowable, under GAAP; it is required under IFRS if the asset's components have "differing patterns of benefit."

Long-lived investment assets are separately defined by the IASB and are normally accounted for on a historical cost basis. In the United States, the FASB does not have a separate definition for property used as an investment only. Property is only held for use or held for sale.

Impairment losses for long-lived assets under GAAP are calculated as the amount of the asset exceeding fair value. Under IFRS, such assets are calculated as the amount an asset exceeds "recoverable amount," or the higher figure between fair value less costs to sell or value in use.

Required Documents for Financial Accounts

Companies that report under IFRS are required to compile and publish a balance sheet, income statement, changes in equity document, cash flow statement, and all associated footnotes. The FASB requires all of these as well and adds in statements about comprehensive income.

Rules vs. Principles

GAAP is considered to be rules-based, meaning rules are made for specific cases and do not necessarily represent a larger principle. IFRS is principles-based and, in that way, more consistent.

Understanding the Cash Flow Statement

The statement of cash flows, or the cash flow statement, is a financial statement that summarizes the amount of cash and cash equivalents entering and leaving a company.

The cash flow statement (CFS) measures how well a company manages its cash position, meaning how well the company generates cash to pay its debt obligations and fund its operating expenses. The cash flow statement complements the balance sheet and income statement and is a mandatory part of a company's financial reports since 1987.

In this article, we will show you how the CFS is structured, and how you can use it when analyzing a company.

Key Takeaways

- A cash flow statement is a financial statement that summarizes the amount of cash and cash equivalents entering and leaving a company.

- The cash flow statement measures how well a company manages its cash position, meaning how well the company generates cash to pay its debt obligations and fund its operating expenses.

- The cash flow statement complements the balance sheet and income statement and is a mandatory part of a company's financial reports since 1987.

- The main components of the cash flow statement are cash from operating activities, cash from investing activities, and cash from financing activities.

- The two methods of calculating cash flow are the direct method and the indirect method.

How to Use a Cash Flow Statement

The CFS allows investors to understand how a company's operations are running, where its money is coming from, and how money is being spent. The CFS is important since it helps investors determine whether a company is on a solid financial footing.

Creditors, on the other hand, can use the CFS to determine how much cash is available (referred to as liquidity) for the company to fund its operating expenses and pay its debts.

The Structure of the Cash Flow Statement

The main components of the cash flow statement are:

1. Cash from operating activities

2. Cash from investing activities

3. Cash from financing activities

4. Disclosure of noncash activities is sometimes included when prepared under the generally accepted accounting principles (GAAP).

It is important to note that the CFS is distinct from the income statement and balance sheet because it does not include the amount of future incoming and outgoing cash that has been recorded on credit. Therefore, cash is not the same as net income, which on the income statement and balance sheet includes cash sales and sales made on credit.

Cash From Operating Activities

The operating activities on the CFS include any sources and uses of cash from business activities. In other words, it reflects how much cash is generated from a company's products or services.

Generally, changes made in cash, accounts receivable, depreciation, inventory, and accounts payable are reflected in cash from operations.

These operating activities might include:

- Receipts from sales of goods and services

- Interest payments

- Income tax payments

- Payments made to suppliers of goods and services used in production

- Salary and wage payments to employees

- Rent payments

- Any other type of operating expenses

In the case of a trading portfolio or an investment company, receipts from the sale of loans, debt, or equity instruments are also included. When preparing a cash flow statement under the indirect method, depreciation, amortization, deferred tax, gains or losses associated with a noncurrent asset, and dividends or revenue received from certain investing activities are also included. However, purchases or sales of long-term assets are not included in operating activities.

What Is a Cash Flow Statement?

How Cash Flow Is Calculated

Cash flow is calculated by making certain adjustments to net income by adding or subtracting differences in revenue, expenses, and credit transactions (appearing on the balance sheet and income statement) resulting from transactions that occur from one period to the next. These adjustments are made because non-cash items are calculated into net income (income statement) and total assets and liabilities (balance sheet). So because not all transactions involve actual cash items, many items have to be re-evaluated when calculating cash flow from operations.

As a result, there are two methods of calculating cash flow: the direct method and the indirect method.

Direct Cash Flow Method

The direct method adds up all the various types of cash payments and receipts, including cash paid to suppliers, cash receipts from customers, and cash paid out in salaries. These figures are calculated by using the beginning and ending balances of a variety of business accounts and examining the net decrease or increase in the accounts.

Indirect Cash Flow Method

With the indirect method, cash flow from operating activities is calculated by first taking the net income off of a company's income statement. Because a company's income statement is prepared on an accrual basis, revenue is only recognized when it is earned and not when it is received.

Net income is not an accurate representation of net cash flow from operating activities, so it becomes necessary to adjust earnings before interest and taxes (EBIT) for items that affect net income, even though no actual cash has yet been received or paid against them. The indirect method also makes adjustments to add back non-operating activities that do not affect a company's operating cash flow.

For example, depreciation is not really a cash expense; it is an amount that is deducted from the total value of an asset that has previously been accounted for. That is why it is added back into net earnings for calculating cash flow.

The only time income from an asset is accounted for in CFS calculations is when the asset is sold.

Accounts Receivable and Cash Flow

Changes in accounts receivable (AR) on the balance sheet from one accounting period to the next must also be reflected in cash flow. If accounts receivable decreases, this implies that more cash has entered the company from customers paying off their credit accounts—the amount by which AR has decreased is then added to net earnings. If accounts receivable increases from one accounting period to the next, the amount of the increase must be deducted from net earnings because, although the amounts represented in AR are revenue, they are not cash.

Inventory Value and Cash Flow

An increase in inventory, on the other hand, signals that a company has spent more money to purchase more raw materials. If the inventory was paid with cash, the increase in the value of inventory is deducted from net earnings. A decrease in inventory would be added to net earnings. If inventory was purchased on credit, an increase in accounts payable would occur on the balance sheet, and the amount of the increase from one year to the other would be added to net earnings.

The same logic holds true for taxes payable, salaries payable, and prepaid insurance. If something has been paid off, then the difference in the value owed from one year to the next has to be subtracted from net income. If there is an amount that is still owed, then any differences will have to be added to net earnings.

Cash From Investing Activities

Investing activities include any sources and uses of cash from a company's investments. A purchase or sale of an asset, loans made to vendors or received from customers, or any payments related to a merger or acquisition is included in this category. In short, changes in equipment, assets, or investments relate to cash from investing.

Usually, cash changes from investing are a "cash out" item, because cash is used to buy new equipment, buildings, or short-term assets such as marketable securities. However, when a company divests an asset, the transaction is considered "cash in" for calculating cash from investing.

Cash From Financing Activities

Cash from financing activities includes the sources of cash from investors or banks, as well as the uses of cash paid to shareholders. Payment of dividends, payments for stock repurchases, and the repayment of debt principal (loans) are included in this category.

Changes in cash from financing are "cash in" when capital is raised, and they are "cash out" when dividends are paid. Thus, if a company issues a bond to the public, the company receives cash financing; however, when interest is paid to bondholders, the company is reducing its cash.

Example of a Cash Flow Statement

Below is an example of a cash flow statement:

From this CFS, we can see that the cash flow for the fiscal year 2017 was $1,522,000. The bulk of the positive cash flow stems from cash earned from operations, which is a good sign for investors. It means that core operations are generating business and that there is enough money to buy new inventory.

The purchasing of new equipment shows that the company has the cash to invest in inventory for growth. Finally, the amount of cash available to the company should ease investors' minds regarding the notes payable, as cash is plentiful to cover that future loan expense.

Negative Cash Flow Statement

Of course, not all cash flow statements look this healthy or exhibit a positive cash flow, but negative cash flow should not automatically raise a red flag without further analysis. Sometimes, negative cash flow is the result of a company's decision to expand its business at a certain point in time, which would be a good thing for the future. This is why analyzing changes in cash flow from one period to the next gives the investor a better idea of how the company is performing, and whether or not a company may be on the brink of bankruptcy or success.

Balance Sheet and Income Statement

As we have already discussed, the cash flow statement is derived from the income statement and the balance sheet. Net earnings from the income statement are the figure from which the information on the CFS is deduced.

As for the balance sheet, the net cash flow in the CFS from one year to the next should equal the increase or decrease of cash between the two consecutive balance sheets that apply to the period that the cash flow statement covers. For example, if you are calculating cash flow for the year 2019, the balance sheets from the years 2018 and 2019 should be used.

The Bottom Line

A cash flow statement is a valuable measure of strength, profitability, and the long-term future outlook for a company. The CFS can help determine whether a company has enough liquidity or cash to pay its expenses. A company can use a cash flow statement to predict future cash flow, which helps with matters of budgeting.

For investors, the cash flow statement reflects a company's financial health since typically the more cash that's available for business operations, the better. However, this is not a fixed rule. Sometimes, a negative cash flow results from a company's growth strategy in the form of expanding its operations.

By studying the cash flow statement, an investor can get a clear picture of how much cash a company generates and gain a solid understanding of the financial well-being of a company.

Breaking Down The Balance Sheet

company's financial statements—balance sheet, income, and cash flow statements—are a key source of data for analyzing the investment value of its stock. Stock investors, both the do-it-yourselfers and those who follow the guidance of an investment professional, don't need to be analytical experts to perform a financial statement analysis. Today, there are numerous sources of independent stock research, online and in print, which can do the "number crunching" for you. However, if you are going to become a serious stock investor, a basic understanding of the fundamentals of financial statement usage is necessary. In this article, we help you to become more familiar with the overall structure of the balance sheet.

The Structure of a Balance Sheet

A company's balance sheet is comprised of assets, liabilities, and equity. Assets represent things of value that a company owns and has in its possession, or something that will be received and can be measured objectively. Liabilities are what a company owes to others—creditors, suppliers, tax authorities, employees, etc. They are obligations that must be paid under certain conditions and time frames. A company's equity represents retained earnings and funds contributed by its shareholders, who accept the uncertainty that comes with ownership risk in exchange for what they hope will be a good return on their investment.

The relationship of these items is expressed in the fundamental balance sheet equation:

Assets = Liabilities + Equity

The meaning of this equation is important. Generally, sales growth, whether rapid or slow, dictates a larger asset base—higher levels of inventory, receivables, and fixed assets (plant, property, and equipment). As a company's assets grow, its liabilities and/or equity also tend to grow in order for its financial position to stay in balance.

How assets are supported, or financed, by a corresponding growth in payables, debt liabilities and equity reveals a lot about a company's financial health. For now, suffice it to say that depending on a company's line of business and industry characteristics, possessing a reasonable mix of liabilities and equity is a sign of a financially healthy company. While it may be an overly simplistic view of the fundamental accounting equation, investors should view a much bigger equity value compared to liabilities as a measure of positive investment quality, because possessing high levels of debt can increase the likelihood that a business will face financial troubles.

Balance Sheet Formats

Standard accounting conventions present the balance sheet in one of two formats: the account form (horizontal presentation) and the report form (vertical presentation). Most companies favor the vertical report form, which does not conform to the typical explanation in investment literature of the balance sheet as having "two sides" that balance out.

Whether the format is up-down or side-by-side, all balance sheets conform to a presentation that positions the various account entries into five sections:

Assets = Liabilities + Equity

• Current assets (short-term): items that are convertible into cash within one year
• Non-current assets (long-term): items of a more permanent nature
As total assets these =
• Current liabilities (short-term): obligations due within one year
• Non-current liabilities (long-term): obligations due beyond one year
These total liabilities +
• Shareholders\' equity (permanent): shareholders\' investment and retained earnings

Account Presentation

In the asset sections mentioned above, the accounts are listed in the descending order of their liquidity (how quickly and easily they can be converted to cash). Similarly, liabilities are listed in the order of their priority for payment. In financial reporting, the terms "current" and "non-current" are synonymous with the terms "short-term" and "long-term," respectively, and are used interchangeably.

It should not be surprising that the diversity of activities included among publicly traded companies is reflected in balance sheet account presentations. The balance sheets of utilities, banks, insurance companies, brokerage and investment banking firms, and other specialized businesses are significantly different in account presentation from those generally discussed in investment literature. In these instances, the investor will have to make allowances and/or defer to the experts.

Lastly, there is little standardization of account nomenclature. For example, even the balance sheet has such alternative names as a "statement of financial position" and "statement of condition." Balance sheet accounts suffer from this same phenomenon. Fortunately, investors have easy access to extensive dictionaries of financial terminology to clarify an unfamiliar account entry.

The Importance of Dates

A balance sheet represents a company's financial position for one day at its fiscal year end, for example, the last day of its accounting period, which can differ from our more familiar calendar year. Companies typically select an ending period that corresponds to a time when their business activities have reached the lowest point in their annual cycle, which is referred to as their natural business year.

In contrast, the income and cash flow statements reflect a company's operations for its whole fiscal year—365 days. Given this difference in "time," when using data from the balance sheet (akin to a photographic snapshot) and the income/cash flow statements (akin to a movie) it is more accurate, and is the practice of analysts, to use an average number for the balance sheet amount. This practice is referred to as "averaging," and involves taking the year-end (2019 and 2020) figures—let's say for total assets—and adding them together and dividing the total by two. This exercise gives us a rough but useful approximation of a balance sheet amount for the whole year 2020, which is what the income statement number, let's say net income, represents. In our example, the number for total assets at year-end 2020 would overstate the amount and distort the return on assets ratio (net income/total assets).

The Bottom Line

Since a company's financial statements are the basis of analyzing the investment value of a stock, this discussion we have completed should provide investors with the "big picture" for developing an understanding of balance sheet basics.

Understanding the Income Statement
What Is the Income Statement?

The income statement is one of three financial statements that stock investors rely on. (The others are the balance sheet and cash flow statement.) Understanding an income statement is essential for investors who want to analyze the profitability and future growth of a company.

Key Takeaways:

- The income statement summarizes a company's revenues and expenses over a period, either quarterly or annually.

- The income statement comes in two forms, multi-step, and single step.

- The multi-step income statement includes four measures of profitability: gross, operating, pretax, and after tax.

- The income statement measures profitability and not cash flow.

In the context of corporate financial reporting, the income statement summarizes a company's revenues (sales) and expenses, quarterly and annually, for the fiscal year. The final net figure and other numbers in the statement are of major interest to investors and analysts.

An Introduction To The Income Statement

Understanding the Income Statement

Income statements come with various monikers. The most commonly used are "statement of income," "statement of earnings," "statement of operations," and "statement of operating results."

Many professionals still use the term P&L, which stands for profit and loss statement, but this term is seldom found in print these days.

The words "profits," "earnings," and "income" all mean the same thing and are used interchangeably.

Two basic formats for the income statement are used in financial reporting–the multi-step and the single-step. These are illustrated below in two examples:

Multi-Step Format	Single-Step Format
Net Sales	Net Sales
Cost of Sales	Materials and Production
Gross Income*	Marketing and Administrative
Selling, General and Administrative Expenses (SG&A)	Research and Development Expenses (R&D)
Operating Income*	Other Income & Expenses

65

Other Income & Expenses	Pretax Income
Pretax Income*	Taxes
Taxes	Net Income
Net Income (after tax)	--

In the multi-step income statement, four measures of profitability (shown with an asterisk*) are revealed at four critical junctions in a company's operations: gross, operating, pretax, and after-tax.

In the single-step presentation, the gross and operating income figures are not stated. They can be calculated from the data provided. In this method, sales minus materials and production equal gross income. By subtracting marketing and administrative and research and development (R&D) expenses from gross income, we get the operating income figure.

Investors must keep in mind that the income statement recognizes revenues when they are realized—that is, when goods are shipped, services rendered, and expenses incurred. With accrual accounting, the flow of accounting events through the income statement does not necessarily coincide with the actual receipt and disbursement of cash. The income statement measures profitability, not cash flow.

Income Statement Accounts (Multi-Step Format)

- Net sales (sales or revenue): This is the value of a company's sales of goods and services to its customers. Although a company's bottom line (its net income) gets most of the attention from investors, the top line is where the revenue or income process begins. In the long run, profit margins on a company's existing products tend to reach a maximum that is difficult to improve upon. Thus, companies typically can grow no faster than their revenues.

- Cost of sales (cost of goods/products sold (COGS), and cost of services): For a manufacturer, the cost of sales is the expense incurred for labor, raw materials, and manufacturing overhead used in the production of goods. While it may be stated separately, depreciation expense belongs in the cost of sales. For wholesalers and retailers, the cost of sales is essentially the purchase cost of merchandise used for resale. For service-related businesses, cost of sales represents the cost of services rendered or cost of revenues.

- Gross profit (gross income or gross margin): A company's gross profit is not just the difference between net sales and the cost of sales. Gross profit also provides the resources to cover all of the company's other expenses. Obviously, the greater and more stable a company's gross margin, the greater potential there is for positive bottom line (net income) results.

- Selling, general, and administrative expenses: Often referred to as SG&A, this is the company's operational expenses. Financial analysts assume that management exercises a great deal of control over this expense category. The trend of SG&A expenses as a percentage of sales is watched closely to detect signs of managerial efficiency, or lack of it.

- Operating income: Deducting SG&A from a company's gross profit produces operating income. This figure represents a company's earnings from its normal operations before any non-operating income and costs such as interest expense, taxes, and special items. Income at the operating level, which is viewed as more dependable, is often used by financial analysts rather than net income as a measure of profitability.

- Interest expense: This item reflects the costs of a company's borrowings. Sometimes, companies record a net figure here for interest expense and interest income from invested funds.

- Pretax income: Another carefully watched indicator of profitability, earnings garnered before the income tax expense is an important bullet in the income statement. Many techniques are available to companies to avoid or minimize taxes that affect their reported income. Because these actions are not part of a company's business operations, analysts may choose to use pretax income as a more accurate measure of corporate profitability.

- Income taxes: As stated, the income tax amount has not actually been paid. This is an estimate or an account that has been created to cover the amount a company expects to pay in taxes.

- Special items or extraordinary expenses: A variety of events can occasion charges against income. They are commonly identified as restructuring charges, unusual or nonrecurring items, and discontinued operations. These write-offs are supposed to be one-time events. Investors need to take these special items into account when making year-to-year profit comparisons because they can distort evaluations.

- Net income (net profit or net earnings): This is the bottom line, which is the most commonly used indicator of a company's profitability. Of course, if expenses exceed income, this account caption will read as a net loss. After the payment of any preferred dividends, net income becomes part of a company's equity position as retained earnings. Supplemental data is also presented for net income based on shares outstanding (basic) and the potential conversion of stock options, warrants, etc. (diluted).

- Comprehensive income: The concept of comprehensive income, which is relatively new,1 takes into consideration the effect of such items as foreign currency translations adjustments, minimum pension liability adjustments, and unrealized gains/losses on certain investments in debt and equity. The investment community continues to focus on the net income figure. The adjustment items all relate to economic events that are out of the control of a company's management. Their impact is real, but they tend to even out over an extended period.

Sample Income Statement

Now let us look at a sample income statement for company XYZ for the fiscal years ending 2019 and 2020 (expenses are in parentheses):

Income Statement For Company XYZ FY 2019 and 2020

(Figures USD)	2019	2020
Net Sales		
Cost of Sales		
Gross Income		
Operating Expenses (SG&A)		
Operating Income	915,000	
Other Income (Expense)	40,000	60,000
Extraordinary Gain (Loss)	-	(15,000)
Interest Expense	(50,000)	(50,000)

Net Profit Before Taxes (Pretax Income)	905,000	
Taxes		
Net Income	605,000	885,000

From the above example, we can deduce that between the years 2019 and 2020, Company XYZ managed to increase sales by about 33% while reducing its cost of sales from 23% to 19% of sales. Consequently, gross income in 2020 increased significantly, which is a huge plus for the company's profitability.

Also, general operating expenses have been kept under strict control, increasing by a modest $25,000. In 2019, the company's operating expenses represented 15.7% of sales, while in 2020, they amounted to only 13%. This is highly favorable in view of the large sales increase.

As a result, the bottom line—net income—for the company increased from $605,000 in 2019 to $885,000 in 2020. The positive year-over-year trends in the statement components, both income and expense, have lifted the company's profit margins (net income/net sales) from 40% to 44%—again, that's highly favorable.

If you are a DIY investor, you will have to do the math. If you use investment research data, the experts crunch the numbers for you.

By understanding the income and expense components of the statement, an investor can appreciate what makes a company profitable. In the case of Company XYZ, it experienced a major increase in sales for the period reviewed and was also able to control the expense side of its business. That is an indicator of efficient management. The one worth further investigation with a view to an investment.

Accountant vs. Financial Planner: What's the Difference?

Accountant vs. Financial Planning: An Overview

Accounting and financial planning provide rewarding and lucrative long-term career options. Both careers offer strong job growth and median incomes higher than the average across all fields.

Both the accountant and financial planning profession are filled with individuals that are bright and motivated while being good with numbers. Interested parties, however, should understand they are quite different, despite both involving heavy doses of numbers and math.

Key Takeaways

- The accountant and financial planner professions tend to rely heavily on math and numbers but there are major differences.

- Accountants do audit work, financial forecasting, and putting together financial statements, while financial planners help individuals with wealth management and retirement planning.

- Accountants are usually meticulous and good with numbers, while financial planners are better at sales and networking.

- Both professions have above average job market outlooks, but accountants are generally paid a salary while much of a financial planners pay is commission based.

Accountant

An accountant records, summarizes, analyzes, and creates reports of financial transactions. Public accountants work for third-party firms auditing financial statements—a legal requirement for any publicly traded company. Internal accountants work for private companies and perform duties such as auditing, inventory accounting, and financial forecasting. Sales is not a part of the job, other than the process of selling oneself and services to potential clients.

Financial Planner

A financial planner is a type of financial advisor who specializes in certain aspects of wealth management, such as tax planning, portfolio management, and retirement planning. While a financial planner must be good with numbers and possess a keen understanding of how the markets work, it is arguably more important to have strong sales and networking skills. Coming

into the profession, one's employer is not likely to hand over clients to manage. Financial planners are tasked with building a book of business on their own.

Key Differences

Required Education

Although neither career imposes specific academic requirements, most successful accountants and financial planners have at least a bachelor's degree. For accountants, the only time a licensing board requires a certain level of education is when pursuing the certified public accountant (CPA) certification.

Becoming a CPA requires 150 hours of post-secondary education, which is more than a bachelor's degree but does not necessarily entail completing a master's degree. Otherwise, individual firms doing the hiring, not state or federal boards, set education requirements for accountants.

Individuals can become a financial planner without a bachelor's degree, as long as they pass the requisite securities exams. However, financial planners often hold specific licenses and designations, the most common being that of a certified financial planner (CFP). A CFP must pass rigorous exams in multiple areas of wealth management and finances. Gaining the CFP designation requires completion of a bachelor's degree from an accredited school.

Necessary Skills

Key accountant skills include being focused, meticulous, and adept with numbers. The work hours are long for the first few years of a public accountant's career. Financial planners are primarily salespeople. Networking is an around-the-clock job for financial planners. Financial planners also tend to enjoy following the markets.

Starting Salaries

Pay structure marks an enormous difference between accounting and financial planning. Accountants receive a straight salary. Bonuses, when applicable, are usually determined by the performance of the firm as a whole. Financial planners, by contrast, receive either a straight commission, charge flat or hourly fees, or receive a mix of commission and fees. It is very much a pay-for-performance career.

For accountants, the Big Four accounting firms—Ernst & Young, Deloitte, KPMG, and

PricewaterhouseCoopers—typically pay entry-level CPA candidates between $60,000 and $80,000 the first year. Beyond the Big Four, starting salary varies greatly depending on the size of the firm, the scope of the job and the region of the country. First-year financial planners are usually offered a small salary or draw, usually between $25,000 and $40,000, as they built their business.

Job Outlook

While the Great Recession battered the financial industry, accounting and financial planning have strong job outlooks for 2019 and beyond. The Bureau of Labor Statistics forecasts greater than 10% growth for accountants and auditors between 2016 and 2026. The projected growth rate for personal financial advisors is 15% in the same period.

Work-Life Balance

Expect a lot of hours your first few years, either as an accountant or financial planner. As an accountant, the busiest months are from January to April, with weekly work hours during those months being upwards of 60. For the remainder of the year, accounting offers a decent work-life balance, with 40-hour work weeks being the standard.

Most financial planners dedicate a lot of hours their first few years to finding and selling clients. This duty alone can push weekly hours worked to above 40. Developing strong word-of-mouth marketing can ease the hours worked significantly.

The Bottom Line

The choice between accounting and financial planning depends more on personality than anything else. Both careers require mathematical proficiency and a strong work ethic. Beyond that, for those that hate sales, financial planning is not a lengthy career choice. Similarly, for those not keen on crunching numbers, preferring to interact with people, accounting will likely come up short as a fulfilling career.

Auditor
What Is an Auditor?

An auditor is a person authorized to review and verify the accuracy of financial records and ensure that companies comply with tax laws. They protect businesses from fraud, point out discrepancies in accounting methods and, on occasion, work on a consultancy basis, helping organizations to spot ways to boost operational efficiency. Auditors work in various capacities within different industries.

Key Takeaways

- The main duty of an auditor is to determine whether financial statements follow generally accepted accounting principles (GAAP).

- The Securities and Exchange Commission (SEC) requires all public companies to conduct regular reviews by external auditors, in compliance with official auditing procedures.

- There are several diverse types of auditors, including those hired to work in-house for companies and those who work for an outside audit firm.

- The final judgment of an audit report can be either qualified or unqualified.

Auditor

Understanding an Auditor

Auditors assess financial operations and ensure that organizations are run efficiently. They are tasked with tracking cash flow from beginning to end and verifying that an organization's funds are properly accounted for.

In the case of public companies, the main duty of an auditor is to determine whether financial statements follow generally accepted accounting principles (GAAP). To meet this requirement, auditors inspect accounting data, financial records, and operational aspects of a business and take detailed notes on each step of the process, known as an audit trail.

Once complete, the auditor's findings are presented in a report that appears as a preface in financial statements. Separate, private reports may also be issued to company management and regulatory authorities as well.

The Securities and Exchange Commission (SEC) demands that the books of all public companies are regularly examined by external, independent auditors, in compliance with official auditing procedures. Official procedures are established by the International Auditing and Assurance Standards Board (IAASB), a committee of the International Federation of Accountants (IFAC).

Unqualified Opinion vs. Qualified Opinion

Auditor reports are usually accompanied by an unqualified opinion. These statements confirm that the company's financial statements conform to GAAP, without providing judgment or an interpretation.

When an auditor is unable to give an unqualified opinion, they will issue a qualified opinion, a statement suggesting that the information provided is limited in scope and/or the company being audited has not maintained GAAP accounting principles.

Auditors assure potential investors that a company's finances are in order and accurate, as well as provide a clear picture of a company's worth to help investors make informed decisions.

Types of Auditors

- Internal auditors are hired by organizations to provide in-house, independent, and objective evaluations of financial and operational business activities, including corporate governance. They report their findings, including tips on how to better run the business, back to senior management.

- External auditors usually work in conjunction with government agencies. They are tasked with providing an objective, public opinion concerning the organization's financial statements and whether they fairly and accurately represent the organization's financial position.

- Government auditors maintain and examine records of government agencies and of private businesses or individuals performing activities subject to government regulations or taxation. Auditors employed through the government ensure revenues are received and spent according to laws and regulations. They detect embezzlement and fraud, analyze agency accounting controls, and evaluate risk management.

- Forensic auditors specialize in crime and are used by law enforcement organizations.

Auditor Qualifications

External auditors working for public accounting firms require a Certified Public Accountant (CPA) license, a professional certification awarded by the American Institute of Certified Public Accountants. In addition to this certification, these auditors also need to obtain state CPA certification. Requirements vary, although most states do demand a CPA designation and two years of professional work experience in public accounting.

Qualifications for internal auditors are less rigorous. Internal auditors are encouraged to get CPA accreditation, although it is not always mandatory. Instead, a bachelor's degree in subjects such as finance and other business disciplines, together with appropriate experience and skills, are often acceptable.

Special Considerations

Auditors are not responsible for transactions that occur after the date of their reports. Moreover, they are not necessarily required to detect all instances of fraud or financial misrepresentation; that responsibility primarily lies with an organization's management team.

Audits are designed to determine whether a company's financial statements are "reasonably stated." In other words, this means that audits do not always cover enough ground to identify cases of fraud. In short, a clean audit offers no guarantee that an organization's accounting is completely legitimate.

Audit
What Is an Audit?

The term audit usually refers to a financial statement audit. A financial audit is an objective examination and evaluation of the financial statements of an organization to make sure that the financial records are a fair and accurate representation of the transactions they claim to represent. The audit can be conducted internally by employees of the organization or externally by an outside Certified Public Accountant (CPA) firm.

Key Takeaways

- There are three main types of audits: external audits, internal audits, and Internal Revenue Service (IRS) audits.

- External audits are commonly performed by Certified Public Accounting (CPA) firms and result in an auditor's opinion which is included in the audit report.

- An unqualified, or clean, audit opinion means that the auditor has not identified any material misstatement because of his or her review of the financial statements.

- External audits can include a review of both financial statements and a company's internal controls.

- Internal audits serve as a managerial tool to make improvements to processes and internal controls.

Audit

Understanding Audits

Almost all companies receive a yearly audit of their financial statements, such as the income statement, balance sheet, and cash flow statement. Lenders often require the results of an external audit annually as part of their debt covenants. For some companies, audits are a legal requirement due to the compelling incentives to intentionally misstate financial information to commit fraud. As a result of the Sarbanes-Oxley Act (SOX) of 2002, publicly traded companies must also receive an evaluation of the effectiveness of their internal controls.

Standards for external audits performed in the United States, called the generally accepted auditing standards (GAAS), are set out by Auditing Standards Board (ASB) of the American Institute of Certified Public Accountants (AICPA). Additional rules for the audits of publicly traded companies are made by the Public Company Accounting Oversight Board (PCAOB), which was established as a result of SOX in 2002. A separate set of international standards, called the International Standards on Auditing (ISA), were set up by the International Auditing and Assurance Standards Board (IAASB).

Types of Audits

External Audits

Audits performed by outside parties can be extremely helpful in removing any bias in reviewing the state of a company's financials. Financial audits seek to identify if there are any material misstatements in the financial statements. An unqualified, or clean, auditor's opinion provides financial statement users with confidence that the financials are both accurate and complete. External audits, therefore, allow stakeholders to make better, more informed decisions related to the company being audited.

External auditors follow a set of standards different from that of the company or organization hiring them to do the work. The biggest difference between an internal and external audit is the concept of independence of the external auditor. When audits are performed by third parties, the resulting auditor's opinion expressed on items being audited (a company's financials, internal controls, or a system) can be candid and honest without it affecting daily work relationships within the company.

Internal Audits

Internal auditors are employed by the company or organization for whom they are performing an audit, and the resulting audit report is given directly to management and the board of directors. Consultant auditors, while not employed internally, use the standards of the company they are auditing as opposed to a separate set of standards. These types of auditors are used when an organization does not have the in-house resources to audit certain parts of their own operations.

The results of the internal audit are used to make managerial changes and improvements to internal controls. The purpose of an internal audit is to ensure compliance with laws and regulations and to help maintain accurate and timely financial reporting and data collection. It also provides a benefit to management by identifying flaws in internal control or financial reporting prior to its review by external auditors.

Internal Revenue Service (IRS) Audits

The Internal Revenue Service (IRS) also routinely performs audits to verify the accuracy of a taxpayer's return and specific transactions. When the IRS audits a person or company, it usually carries a negative connotation and is seen as evidence of some type of wrongdoing by the taxpayer. However, being selected for an audit is not necessarily indicative of any wrongdoing.

IRS audit selection is usually made by random statistical formulas that analyze a taxpayer's return and compare it to similar returns. A taxpayer may also be selected for an audit if they have any dealings with another person or company who was found to have tax errors on their audit.

There are three IRS audit outcomes available: no change to the tax return, a change that is accepted by the taxpayer, or a change that the taxpayer disagrees with. If the change is accepted, the taxpayer may owe additional taxes or penalties. If the taxpayer disagrees, there is a process to follow that may include mediation or an appeal.

Tax Accounting
What Is Tax Accounting?

Tax accounting is a structure of accounting methods focused on taxes rather than the appearance of public financial statements. Tax accounting is governed by the Internal Revenue Code, which dictates the specific rules that companies and individuals must follow when preparing their tax returns.

Key Takeaways

- Tax accounting is the subsector of accounting that deals with the preparations of tax returns and tax payments.

- Tax accounting is used by individuals, businesses, corporations, and other entities.

- Tax accounting for an individual focuses on income, qualifying deductions, donations, and any investment gains or losses.

- For a business, tax accounting is more complex, with greater scrutiny regarding how funds are spent and what is or is not taxable.

Understanding Tax Accounting

Tax accounting is the means of accounting for tax purposes. It applies to everyone—individuals, businesses, corporations, and other entities. Even those who are exempt from paying taxes must participate in tax accounting. The purpose of tax accounting is to be able to track funds (funds coming in as well as funds going out) associated with individuals and entities.

Tax Accounting Principles vs. Financial Accounting (GAAP)

In the United States, there are two sets of principles that are used when it comes to accounting. The first is tax accounting principles and the second is financial accounting, or accepted accounting principles (GAAP).

Under GAAP, companies must follow a common set of accounting principles, standards, and procedures when they compile their financial statements by accounting for any and all financial transactions. Balance sheet items can be accounted for differently when preparing financial statements and tax payables. For example, companies can prepare their financial statements implementing the first-in-first-out (FIFO) method to record their inventory for financial purposes, yet they can implement the last-in-first-out (LIFO) approach for tax purposes. The latter procedure reduces the current year's taxes payable.

While accounting encompasses all financial transactions to some degree, tax accounting focuses solely on those transactions that affect an entity's tax burden, and how those items relate to proper tax calculation and tax document preparation. Tax accounting is regulated by the Internal Revenue Service (IRS) to ensure that all associated tax laws are adhered to by tax accounting professionals and individual taxpayers. The IRS also requires the use of specific documents and forms to properly submit tax information as required by law.

Hiring a professional tax accountant is optional for an individual, but often necessary for a corporation, as business taxes are more complicated than personal taxes.

Types of Tax Accounting

Tax Accounting for an Individual

For an individual taxpayer, tax accounting focuses solely on items such as income, qualifying deductions, investment gains or losses, and other transactions that affect the individual's tax burden. This limits the amount of information that is necessary for an individual to manage an annual tax return, and while a tax accountant can be used by an individual, it is not a legal requirement.

Meanwhile, general accounting would involve the tracking of all funds coming in and out of the persons' possession regardless of the purpose, including personal expenses that have no tax implications.

Tax Accounting for a Business

From a business perspective, more information must be analyzed as part of the tax accounting process. While the company's earnings, or incoming funds, must be tracked just as they are for the individual, there is an additional level of complexity regarding any outgoing funds directed towards certain business obligations. This can include funds directed towards specific business expenses as well as funds directed towards shareholders.

While it is also not required that a business use a tax accountant to perform these duties, it is common in larger organizations due to the complexity of the records involved.

Even legally tax-exempt organizations use tax accounting as they are required to file annual returns.

Tax Accounting for a Tax-Exempt Organization

Even in instances where an organization is tax-exempt, tax accounting is necessary. This is due to the fact that most organizations must file annual returns. They must provide information regarding any incoming funds, such as grants or donations, as well as how the funds are used during the organization's operation. This helps ensure that the organization adheres to all laws and regulations governing the proper operation of a tax-exempt entity.

Forensic Accounting

What Is Forensic Accounting?

Forensic accounting utilizes accounting, auditing, and investigative skills to conduct an examination into the finances of an individual or business. Forensic accounting provides an accounting analysis suitable to be used in legal proceedings. Forensic accountants are trained to look beyond the numbers and deal with the business reality of a situation. Forensic accounting is frequently used in fraud and embezzlement cases to explain the nature of a financial crime in court.

Key Takeaways

- Forensic accounting is a combination of accounting and investigative techniques used to discover financial crimes.

- One of the key functions of forensic accounting is to explain the nature of a financial crime to the courts.

- Forensic accounting entails the use of tracing funds, asset identification, asset recovery, and due diligence reviews

- Forensic accounting is used by the insurance industry to establish damages from claims.

Understanding Forensic Accounting

Forensic accountants analyze, interpret, and summarize complex financial and business matters. They may be employed by insurance companies, banks, police forces, government agencies, or public accounting firms. Forensic accountants compile financial evidence, develop computer applications to manage the information collected, and communicate their findings in the form of reports or presentations.

Along with testifying in court, a forensic accountant may be asked to prepare visual aids to support trial evidence. For business investigations, forensic accounting entails the use of tracing funds, asset identification, asset recovery, and due diligence reviews. Forensic accountants may seek out additional training in alternative dispute resolution (ADR) due to their high level of involvement in legal issues and familiarity with the judicial system.

Forensic Accounting for Litigation Support

Forensic accounting is utilized in litigation when quantification of damages is needed. Parties involved in legal disputes use the quantifications to assist in resolving disputes via settlements or court decisions. For example, this may arise due to compensation and benefit disputes. The forensic accountant may be utilized as an expert witness if the dispute escalates to a court decision.

Forensic Accounting for Criminal Investigation

Forensic accounting is also used to discover whether a crime occurred and assess the likelihood of criminal intent. Such crimes may include employee theft, securities fraud, falsification of financial statement information, identity theft, or insurance fraud.

Forensic accounting is often brought to bear in complex and high-profile financial crimes. For instance, the scope and mechanics of Bernie Madoff's Ponzi scheme is understood today because forensic accountants dissected the scheme and made it understandable for the court case.

Forensic accountants may also assist in searching for hidden assets in divorce cases or provide their services for other civil matters such as breach of contracts, tort, disagreements relating to company acquisitions, breaches of warranty, or business valuation disputes.

Forensic accounting assignments can include investigating construction claims, expropriations, product liability claims, or trademark or patent infringements. And, if all that wasn't enough, forensic accounting may also be used to determine the economic results of the breach of a nondisclosure or non-compete agreement.

Forensic Accounting in the Insurance Industry

Forensic accounting is routinely used by the insurance industry. In this capacity, a forensic accountant may be asked to quantify the economic damages arising from a vehicle accident, a case of medical malpractice, or some other claim. One of the concerns about taking a forensic accounting approach to insurance claims as opposed to an adjuster approach is that forensic accounting is mainly concerned with historical data and may miss relevant current information that changes the assumptions around the claim.

Chart of Accounts (COA)
What Is a Chart of Accounts (COA)?

A chart of accounts (COA) is an index of all the financial accounts in the general ledger of a company. In short, it is an organizational tool that provides a digestible breakdown of all the financial transactions that a company conducted during a specific accounting period, broken down into subcategories.

Key Takeaways

- A chart of accounts (COA) is a financial organizational tool that provides a complete listing of every account in the general ledger of a company, broken down into subcategories.

- It is used to organize finances and give interested parties, such as investors and shareholders, a clearer insight into a company's financial health.

- To make it easier for readers to locate specific accounts, each chart of accounts typically contains a name, brief description, and an identification code.

How Charts of Accounts (COA) Works

Companies use a chart of accounts (COA) to organize their finances and give interested parties, such as investors and shareholders, a clearer insight into their financial health. Separating expenditures, revenue, assets, and liabilities help to achieve this and ensure that financial statements are in compliance with reporting standards.

The list of each account a company owns is typically shown in the order the accounts appear in its financial statements. That means that balance sheet accounts, assets, liabilities, and shareholders' equity are listed first, followed by accounts in the income statement — revenues and expenses.

For a small corporation, COAs might include these sub-accounts under the assets account:

- Cash

- Savings account

- Petty cash balance

- Accounts receivable

- Undeposited funds

- Inventory assets

- Prepaid insurance

- Vehicles

- Buildings

Liabilities account may have sub-accounts, such as:

- The company credit card

- Accrued liabilities

- Accounts payable

- Payroll liabilities

- Notes payable

Shareholders' equity can be broken down into the following accounts:

- Common stock

- Preferred stock

- Retained earnings

To make it easier for readers to locate specific accounts, each chart of accounts typically contains a name, brief description, and an identification code. Each chart in the list is assigned a multi-digit number; all asset accounts start with the number 1, for example.

Here is a way to think about how COAs relate to your own finances. Say you have a checking account, a savings account, and a certificate of deposit (CD) at the same bank. When you log in to your account online, you will typically go to an overview page that shows the balance in each account. Similarly, if you use an online program that helps you manage all your accounts in one place, like Mint or Personal Capital, what you're looking at is basically the same thing as a company's COA. You can see all your assets and liabilities, all on one page.

Example of a COA

Within the accounts of the income statement, revenues and expenses could be broken into operating revenues, operating expenses, non-operating revenues, and non-operating losses. In addition, the operating revenues and operating expenses accounts might be further organized by business function and/or by company divisions.

Many organizations structure their COA so that expense information is separately compiled by department; thus, the sales department, engineering department, and accounting department all have the same set of expense accounts. Examples of expense accounts include the cost of goods sold (COGS), depreciation expense, utility expense, and wages expense.

Special Considerations

COAs can differ and be tailored to reflect a company's operations. However, they also must respect the guidelines set out by the Financial Accounting Standards Board (FASB) and generally accepted accounting principles (GAAP).

Of crucial importance is that COAs are kept the same from year to year. Doing so ensures that accurate comparisons of the company's finances can be made over time.

Journal
What Is a Journal?

A journal is a detailed account that records all the financial transactions of a business, to be used for the future reconciling of accounts and the transfer of information to other official accounting records, such as the general ledger. A journal states the date of a transaction, which accounts were affected, and the amounts, usually in a double-entry bookkeeping method.

Key Takeaways

- A journal is a detailed record of all the transactions done by a business.

- Reconciling accounts and transferring information to other accounting records is done using the information recorded in a journal.

- When a transaction is recorded in a company's journal, it is usually recorded using a double entry method, but can also be recorded using a single-entry method of bookkeeping.

- The double-entry method reflects changes in two accounts after a transaction has occurred: an increase in one and a decrease in the corresponding account.

- Single-entry bookkeeping is rarely used and only notes changes in one account.

- A journal is also used in the financial world to refer to a trading journal that details the trades made by an investor and why.

Understanding a Journal

For accounting purposes, a journal is a physical record or digital document kept as a book, spreadsheet, or data within accounting software. When a business transaction is made, a bookkeeper enters the financial transaction as a journal entry. If the expense or income affects one or more business accounts, the journal entry will detail that as well.

Journaling is an essential part of objective record-keeping and allows for concise reviews and records-transfer later in the accounting process. Journals are often reviewed as part of a trade or audit process, along with the general ledger.

Typical information that is recorded in a journal includes sales, expenses, movements of cash, inventory, and debt. It is advised to record this information as it happens as opposed to later so that the information is recorded accurately without any guesswork later.

Having an accurate journal is not only important for the success of a business, by spotting errors and budgeting correctly, but is also imperative when taxes are filed.

Using Double-Entry Bookkeeping in Journals

Double-entry bookkeeping is the most generic form of accounting. It directly affects the way journals are kept and how journal entries are recorded. Every business transaction is made up of an exchange between two accounts.

This means that each journal entry is recorded with two columns. For example, if a business owner purchases $1,000 worth of inventory with cash, the bookkeeper records two transactions in a journal entry. The cash account decreases by $1,000, and the inventory account, which is a current asset, increases by $1,000.

Using Single-Entry Bookkeeping in Journals

Single-entry bookkeeping is rarely used in accounting and business. It is the most basic form of accounting and is set up like a checkbook, in that there is only a single account used for each journal entry. It is a simple running total of cash inflows and cash outflows.

If, for example, a business owner purchases $1,000 worth of inventory with cash, the single-entry system records a $1,000 reduction in cash, with the total ending balance below it. It is possible to separate income and expenses into two columns so a business can track total income and total expenses, and not just the aggregate ending balance.

The Journal in Investing and Trading

A journal is also used in the investment finance sector. For an individual investor or professional manager, a journal is a comprehensive and detailed record of trades occurring in the investor's own accounts, which is used for tax, evaluation, and auditing purposes.

Traders use journals to keep a quantifiable chronicle of their trading performance over time to learn from past successes and failures. Although past performance is not a predictor of future performance, a trader can use a journal to learn as much as possible from their trading history, including the emotional elements as to why a trader may have gone against their chosen strategy.

The journal typically has a record of profitable trades, unprofitable trades, watch lists, pre- and post-market records, notes on why an investment was purchased or sold, and so on.

Double Entry Definition
What Is Double Entry?

Double entry, a fundamental concept underlying present-day bookkeeping and accounting, states that every financial transaction has equal and opposite effects in at least two different accounts. It is used to satisfy the accounting equation:

Assets = Liabilities + Equity{aligned} &{Assets} = {Liabilities} + {Equity} {aligned}Assets = Liabilities + Equity

With a double entry system, credits are offset by debits in a general ledger or T-account.

Double Entry

The Basics of Double Entry

In the double-entry system, transactions are recorded in terms of debits and credits. Since a debit in one account offsets a credit in another, the sum of all debits must equal the sum of all credits. The double-entry system of bookkeeping standardizes the accounting process and improves the accuracy of prepared financial statements, allowing for improved detection of errors.

Types of Accounts

Bookkeeping and accounting are ways of measuring, recording, and communicating a firm's financial information. A business transaction is an economic event that is recorded for accounting/bookkeeping purposes. In general terms, it is a business interaction between economic entities, such as customers and businesses or vendors and businesses.

Under the systematic process of accounting, these interactions are classified into accounts. There are seven diverse types of accounts that all business transactions can be classified:

- Assets

- Liabilities

- Equities

- Revenue

- Expenses

- Gains

- Losses

Bookkeeping and accounting track changes in each account as a company continues operations.

Debits and Credits

Debits and credits are essential to the double entry system. In accounting, a debit refers to an entry on the left side of an account ledger, and credit refers to an entry on the right side of an account ledger. To be in balance, the total of debits and credits for a transaction must be equal. Debits do not always equate to increases and credits do not always equate to decreases.

A debit may increase one account while decreasing another. For example, a debit increases asset accounts but decreases liability and equity accounts, which supports the general accounting equation of Assets = Liabilities + Equity. On the income statement, debits increase the balances in expense and loss accounts, while credits decrease their balances. Debits decrease revenue and gains account balances, while credits increase their balances.

The Double-Entry Accounting System

Double-entry bookkeeping was developed in the mercantile period of Europe to help rationalize commercial transactions and make trade more efficient. It also helped merchants and bankers understand their costs and profits. Some thinkers have argued that double-entry accounting was a key calculative technology responsible for the birth of capitalism.

The accounting equation forms the foundation of the double-entry accounting and is a concise representation of a concept that expands into the complex, expanded and multi-item display of the balance sheet. The balance sheet is based on the double-entry accounting system where total assets of a company are equal to the total of liabilities and shareholder equity.

The representation equates all uses of capital (assets) to all sources of capital (where debt capital leads to liabilities and equity capital leads to shareholders' equity). For a company keeping accurate accounts, every single business transaction will be represented in at least of its two accounts.

For instance, if a business takes a loan from a financial entity like a bank, the borrowed money will raise the company's assets and the loan liability will also rise by an equivalent amount. If a business buys raw material by paying cash, it will lead to an increase in the inventory (asset) while reducing cash capital (another asset). Because there are two or more accounts affected by every transaction conducted by a company, the accounting system is referred to as double-entry accounting.

This practice ensures that the accounting equation always remains balanced – that is, the left side value of the equation will always match with the right-side value.

Key Takeaways

- Double entry refers to an accounting concept whereby assets = liabilities + owners' equity.

- In the double-entry system, transactions are recorded in terms of debits and credits.

- Double-entry bookkeeping was developed in the mercantile period of Europe to help rationalize commercial transactions and make trade more efficient.

- The emergence of double entry has been linked to the birth of capitalism.

Real World Example of Double Entry

A bakery purchases a fleet of refrigerated delivery trucks on credit; the total credit purchase was $250,000. The new set of trucks will be used in business operations and will not be sold for at least 10 years—their estimated useful life.

To account for the credit purchase, entries must be made in their respective accounting ledgers. Because the business has accumulated more assets, a debit to the asset account for the cost of the purchase ($250,000) will be made. To account for the credit purchase, a credit entry of $250,000 will be made to notes payable. The debit entry increases the asset balance, and the credit entry increases the notes payable liability balance by the same amount.

Double entries can also occur within the same class. If the bakery's purchase was made with cash, a credit would be made to cash and a debit to asset, still resulting in a balance.

Debit
What Is a Debit?

A debit is an accounting entry that results in either an increase in assets or a decrease in liabilities on a company's balance sheet. In fundamental accounting, debits are balanced by credits, which operate in the exact opposite direction.

For instance, if a firm takes out a loan to purchase equipment, it will debit fixed assets and at the same time credit a liabilities account, depending on the nature of the loan. The abbreviation for debit is sometimes "dry," which is short for "debtor."

Debit

How Debits Work

A debit is a feature found in all double-entry accounting systems. In a standard journal entry, all debits are placed as the top lines, while all credits are listed on the line below debits. When using T-accounts, a debit is the left side of the chart while a credit is the right side.

Debits and credits are utilized in the trial balance and adjusted trial balance to ensure all entries balance. The total dollar amount of all debits must equal the total dollar amount of all credits. In other words, finances must balance.

A dangling debit is a debit balance with no offsetting credit balance that would allow it to be written off. It occurs in financial accounting and reflects discrepancies in a company's balance sheet, and when a company purchases goodwill or services to create a debit.

As a quick example, if Barnes & Noble sold $20,000 worth of books, it would debit its cash account $20,000 and credit its books or inventory account $20,000. This double-entry system shows that the company now has $20,000 more in cash and a corresponding $20,000 less in books.

Normal Accounting Balances

Certain types of accounts have natural balances in financial accounting systems. Assets and expenses have natural debit balances. This means positive values for assets and expenses are debited and negative balances are credited.

For example, upon the receipt of $1,000 cash, a journal entry would include a debit of $1,000 to the cash account in the balance sheet, because cash is increasing. If another transaction involves payment of $500 in cash, the journal entry would have a credit to the cash account of $500 because cash is being reduced. In effect, a debit increases an expense account in the income statement, and a credit decreases it.

Liabilities, revenues, and equity accounts have natural credit balances. If a debit is applied to any of these accounts, the account balance has decreased. For example, a debit to the accounts payable account in the balance sheet indicates a reduction of a liability. The offsetting credit is a credit to cash because the reduction of a liability means the debt is being paid and cash is an outflow. For the revenue accounts in the income statement, debit entries decrease the account, while a credit points to an increase to the account.

The concept of debits and offsetting credits are the cornerstone of double-entry accounting.

Debit Notes

Debit notes are a form of proof that one business has created a legitimate debit entry while dealing with another business (B2B). This might occur when a purchaser returns materials to a supplier and needs to validate the reimbursed amount. In this case, the purchaser issues a debit note reflecting the accounting transaction.

A business might issue a debit note in response to a received credit note. Mistakes (often interest charges and fees) in a sales, purchase, or loan invoice might prompt a firm to issue a debit note to help correct the error.

A debit note or debit receipt is remarkably like an invoice. The main difference is that invoices always show a sale, where debit notes and debit receipts reflect adjustments or returns on transactions that have already taken place.

Key Takeaways

- A debit is an accounting entry that creates a decrease in liabilities or an increase in assets.

- In double-entry bookkeeping, all debits must be offset with corresponding credits in their T-accounts.

- On a balance sheet, positive values for assets and expenses are debited, and negative balances are credited.

Margin Debit

When buying on margin, investors borrow funds from their brokerage and then combine those funds with their own to purchase a greater number of shares than they would have been able to purchase with their own funds. The debit amount recorded by the brokerage in an investor's account represents the cash cost of the transaction to the investor.

The debit balance, in a margin account, is the amount of money owed by the customer to the broker (or another lender) for funds advanced to purchase securities. The debit balance is the amount of funds the customer must put into his or her margin account, following the successful execution of a security purchase order, to properly settle the transaction.

The debit balance can be contrasted with the credit balance. While a long margin position has a debit balance, a margin account with only short positions will show a credit balance. The credit balance is the sum of the proceeds from a short sale and the required margin amount under Regulation T.

Sometimes, a trader's margin account has both long and short margin positions. Adjusted debit balance is the amount in a margin account that is owed to the brokerage firm, minus profits on short sales and balances in a special miscellaneous account (SMA).

Contra Accounts

Certain accounts are used for valuation purposes and are displayed on the financial statements opposite the normal balances. These accounts are called contra accounts. The debit entry to a contra account has the opposite effect as it would to a normal account.

For example, an allowance for uncollectable accounts offsets the asset accounts receivable. Because the allowance is a negative asset, a debit decreases the allowance. A contra asset's debit is the opposite of a normal account's debit, which increases the asset.

Debit Cards vs. Credit Cards

Credit cards and debit cards typically look almost identical, with 16-digit card numbers, expiration dates, and personal identification number (PIN) codes. But that is where the similarity ends.

Debit cards allow bank customers to spend money by drawing on existing funds they have already deposited at the bank, such as from a checking account. The first debit card may have hit the market as early as 1966 when the Bank of Delaware piloted the idea.3

Credit cards allow consumers to borrow money from the card issuer up to a certain limit to purchase items or withdraw cash. Debit cards offer the convenience of credit cards and many of the same consumer protections when issued by major payment processors like Visa or MasterCard.

Credit
What Is Credit?

How do you define credit? This term has many meanings in the financial world, but credit is defined as a contract agreement in which a borrower receives a sum of money or something of value and repays the lender later, with interest.

Credit also may refer to the creditworthiness or credit history of an individual or a company. To an accountant, it refers to a bookkeeping entry that either decreases assets or increases liabilities and equity on a company's balance sheet.

Key Takeaways

- Credit is defined as an agreement between a lender and a borrower.

- Credit also refers to an individual or business' creditworthiness or credit history.

- In accounting, a credit may either decrease assets or increase liabilities as well as decrease expenses or increase revenue.

How Credit Works

In its first and most common-used definition, credit refers to an agreement to purchase a product or service with the express promise to pay for it later. This is known as buying on credit.

The most generic form of buying on credit today is via the use of credit cards. This introduces a middleperson to the credit agreement: the bank that issued the card repays the merchant in full and extends credit to the buyer, who may repay the bank over time.

The amount of money a consumer or business has available to borrow—or their creditworthiness—is also called credit. For example, someone may say, "They have excellent credit, so they are not worried about the bank rejecting their mortgage application."

Finally, in accounting, credit is an entry that records a decrease in assets or an increase in liability as well as a decrease in expenses or an increase in revenue. So, a credit increases net income on the company's income statement, while a debit reduces net income.

Service credit is an agreement between a consumer and a service provider such as a utility, cell phone, or cable company.

Credit

Types of Credit

There are many different forms of credit. The most popular form is bank credit or financial credit. This kind of credit includes car loans, mortgages, signature loans, and lines of credit. When the bank lends to a consumer, it credits money to the borrower, who must pay it back at a future date.

In other cases, credit can refer to a reduction in the amount one owes. For example, imagine someone owes their credit card company a total of $1,000 but returns one purchase worth $300 to the store. The return will be recorded as a credit on the account, reducing the amount owed to $700.

For example, when a consumer uses a Visa card to make a purchase, the card is considered a form of credit because the consumer is buying goods with the understanding that they will pay the bank back later.

Financial resources are not the only form of credit that may be offered. There may be an exchange of goods and services in exchange for a deferred payment, which is another type of credit.

When suppliers give products or services to an individual but do not require payment until later, that is a form of credit. When a restaurant accepts a truckload of food from a vendor who bills the restaurant a month later, the vendor is offering the restaurant a form of credit.

Special Considerations

In the context of personal banking, a credit is an entry recording a sum that has been received. Traditionally, credits (deposits) appear on the right-hand side of a checking account register, and debits (money spent) appear on the left.

From a financial accounting perspective, if a company buys something on credit, its accounts must record the transaction several places in its balance sheet. To explain, imagine that a company buys merchandise on credit.

After the purchase, the company's inventory account increases by the amount of the purchase (via a debit), adding an asset to the company. However, its accounts payable field also increases by the amount of the purchase (via a credit), adding a liability to the company.

Closing Entry
What Is a Closing Entry?

A closing entry is a journal entry made at the end of accounting periods that involves shifting data from temporary accounts on the income statement to permanent accounts on the balance sheet. Temporary accounts include revenue, expenses, and dividends, and these accounts must be closed at the end of the accounting year.

Key Takeaways:

- A closing entry is a journal entry made at the end of the accounting period.

- It involves shifting data from temporary accounts on the income statement to permanent accounts on the balance sheet.

- All income statement balances are eventually transferred to retained earnings.

How to Make a Closing Entry

Understanding Closing Entries

The purpose of the closing entry is to reset the temporary account balances to zero on the general ledger, the record-keeping system for a company's financial data.

Temporary accounts are used to record accounting activity during a specific period. All revenue and expense accounts must end with a zero balance because they are reported in defined periods and are not carried over into the future. For example, $100 in revenue this year does not count as $100 of revenue for next year, even if the company retained the funds for use in the next 12 months.

Permanent accounts, on the other hand, track activities that extend beyond the current accounting period. They are housed on the balance sheet, a section of the financial statements that gives investors an indication of a company's value, including its assets and liabilities.

Any account listed on the balance sheet, barring paid dividends, is a permanent account. On the balance sheet, $75 of cash held today is still valued at $75 next year, even if it is not spent.

As part of the closing entry process, the net income (NI) is moved into retained earnings on the balance sheet. The assumption is that all income from the company in one year is held onto for future use. Any funds that are not held onto incur an expense that reduces NI. One such expense that is determined at the end of the year is dividends. The last closing entry reduces the amount retained by the amount paid out to investors.

Income Summary Account

Temporary account balances can either be shifted directly to the retained earnings account or to an intermediate account known as the income summary account beforehand.

Income summary is a holding account used to aggregate all income accounts except for dividend expenses. Income summary is not reported on any financial statements because it is only used during the closing process, and at the end of the closing process the account balance is zero.

Income summary effectively collects NI for the period and distributes the amount to be retained into retained earnings. Balances from temporary accounts are shifted to the income summary account first to leave an audit trail for accountants to follow.

Recording a Closing Entry

There is an established sequence of journal entries that encompass the entire closing procedure:

1. First, all revenue accounts are transferred to income summary. This is done through a journal entry debiting all revenue accounts and crediting income summary.

2. Next, the same process is performed for expenses. All expenses are closed out by crediting the expense accounts and debiting income summary.

3. Third, the income summary account is closed and credited to retained earnings.

4. Finally, if a dividend was paid out, the balance is transferred from the dividends account to retained earnings.

Modern accounting software automatically generates closing entries.

Special Considerations

If a company's revenues are greater than its expenses, the closing entry entails debiting income summary and crediting retained earnings. In the event of a loss for the period, the income summary account needs to be credited and retained earnings reduced through a debit.

Finally, dividends are closed directly to retained earnings. The retained earnings account is reduced by the amount paid out in dividends through a debit, and the dividends expense is credited.

Invoice
What Is an Invoice?

An invoice is a time-stamped commercial document that itemizes and records a transaction between a buyer and a seller. If goods or services were purchased on credit, the invoice usually specifies the terms of the deal and provides information on the available methods of payment.

Types of invoices may include a paper receipt, a bill of sale, debit note, sales invoice, or online electronic record.

Key Takeaways

- An invoice is a document that maintains a record of a transaction between a buyer and seller, such as a paper receipt from a store or online record from an e-tailer.

- Invoices are a critical element of accounting internal controls and audits.

- Charges found on an invoice must be approved by the responsible management personnel.

- Invoices outline payment terms, unit costs, shipping, handling, and any other terms outlined during the transaction.

Invoice

The Basics of an Invoice

An invoice must state it is an invoice on the face of the bill. It typically has a unique identifier called the invoice number that is useful for internal and external reference. An invoice typically contains contact information for the seller or service provider in case there is an error relating to the billing.

Payment terms may be outlined on the invoice, as well as the information relating to any discounts, prompt payment details or finance charges assessed for overdue payments. It also presents the unit cost of an item, total units purchased, freight, handling, shipping, and associated tax charges, and it outlines the total amount owed.

Companies may opt to simply send a month-end statement as the invoice for all outstanding transactions. If this is the case, the statement must indicate that no subsequent invoices will be sent. Historically, invoices have been recorded on paper, often with multiple copies generated so that the buyer and seller each have a record of the transaction for their own records. Currently, computer-generated invoices are quite common. They can be printed to paper on demand or sent by email to the parties of a transaction. Electronic records also allow for easier searching and sorting of transactions or specific dates.

A pro forma invoice is a preliminary bill of sale sent to buyers in advance of a shipment or delivery of goods. The invoice will typically describe the purchased items and other valuable information such as the shipping weight and transport charges. Pro forma invoices often come into play with international transactions, especially for customs purposes on imports.

A pro-forma invoice is a binding agreement, although the terms of sale are subject to change.

The Importance of Invoice Date

The invoice date represents the time-stamped time and date on which the goods have been billed and the transaction officially recorded. Therefore, the invoice date has essential information regarding payment, as it dictates the credit duration and due date of the bill. This is especially crucial for entities offering credit, such as net 30. The actual due date of the invoice is usually 30 days after the invoice date. Likewise, companies offer customers the option to return items typically have a deadline based on a certain number of days since proof of purchase, as indicated on the invoice.

E-Invoicing

Since the advent of the computer era, people and businesses have found it easier to rely on electronic invoicing as an alternative to paper documents. Electronic invoicing, or e-invoicing, is a form of electronic billing to generate, store and monitor transaction-related documents between parties and ensure the terms of their agreements are fulfilled.

These e-documents may include invoices and receipts, purchase orders, debit and credit notes, payment terms and instructions, and remittance slips. Digital invoices are normally sent via email, web page or app. Advantages include the following:

- Permanence and resistance to physical damage

- Ease of searching and sorting for specific names, terms, or dates

- Increased auditability

- The ability to print or reproduce on demand

- The ability for data collection and business intelligence

- Reduction of paper use

E-invoicing includes several technologies and entry options and is used as a general term to describe any method by which an invoice is electronically presented to a customer for payment. Several e-invoicing standards, such as EDIFACT and UBL, have been developed around to world to facilitate adoption and efficiency.

Invoices and Accounts Payable

Invoices track the sale of a product for inventory control, accounting and tax purposes, which help keep track of accounts payable and similar obligations due. Many companies ship the product and expect payment on a later date, so the total amount due becomes an account payable for the buyer and an account receivable for the seller.

Modern-day invoices are transmitted electronically, rather than being paper based. If an invoice is lost, the buyer may request a copy from the seller. The use of an invoice represents the presence of credit, as the seller has sent a product or provided a service without receiving cash up front.

Invoices are different from purchase orders, which are created before a customer order a good or service.

Invoices and Internal Controls

Invoices are a critical element of accounting internal controls. Charges on an invoice must be approved by the responsible management personnel. Alternatively, an invoice is matched to a purchase order, and upon reconciling the information, payment is made for approved transactions. An auditing firm ensures invoices are entered into the appropriate accounting period when testing for expense cutoff.

Introduction to Accounting Information Systems (AIS)

An accounting information system (AIS) is a structure that a business uses to collect, store, manage, process, retrieve, and report its financial data so it can be used by accountants, consultants, business analysts, managers, chief financial officers (CFOs), auditors, regulators, and tax agencies.

Specially trained accountants work in-depth with AIS to ensure the highest level of accuracy in a company's financial transactions and record-keeping, as well as make financial data easily available to those who legitimately need access to it—all while keeping data intact and secure.

Key Takeaways

- An accounting information system (AIS) is used by companies to collect, store, manage, process, retrieve, and report financial data.

- AIS can be used by accountants, consultants, business analysts, managers, chief financial officers, auditors, and regulators.

- An AIS helps the different departments within a company work together.

- An effective AIS uses hardware and software to effectively store and retrieve data.

- The internal and external controls of an AIS are critical to protecting a company's sensitive data.

Introduction To Accounting Information Systems

Understanding Accounting Information Systems (AIS)

An accounting information system is a way of tracking all accounting and business activity for a company. Accounting information systems consist of six primary components: people, procedures and instructions, data, software, information technology infrastructure, and internal controls. Below is a breakdown of each component in detail.

1. AIS People

The people in an AIS are the system users. An AIS helps the different departments within a company work together. Professionals who may need to use an organization's AIS include:

- Accountants

- Consultants

- Business analysts

- Managers

- Chief financial officers

- Auditors

For example, management can establish sales goals for which staff can then order the appropriate amount of inventory. The inventory order notifies the accounting department of a new payable. When sales are made in a business, the people and departments involved in the sales process could include the following:

5. Salespeople enter the customer orders into the AIS.

6. Accounting bills or sends an invoice to the customer.

7. The warehouse assembles the order.

8. The shipping department sends the order out to the customer.

9. The accounting department gets notified of a new accounts receivable, which is an IOU from the customer that's typically paid within 30, 60, or 90 days.

10. The customer service department tracks the order and customer shipments.

11. Management uses AIS to create sales reports and perform cost analysis, which can include inventory, shipping, and manufacturing costs.

With a well-designed AIS, everyone within an organization can access the same system and retrieve the same information. An AIS also simplifies the process of reporting information to people outside of the organization, when necessary.

For example, consultants might use the information in an AIS to analyze the effectiveness of the company's pricing structure by looking at cost data, sales data, and revenue. Also, auditors can use the data to assess a company's internal controls, financial condition, and compliance with regulations such as the Sarbanes-Oxley Act (SOX).

The AIS should be designed to meet the needs of the people who will be using it. The system should also be easy to use and should improve, not hinder efficiency.

2. Procedures and Instructions

The procedure and instructions of an AIS are the methods it uses for collecting, storing, retrieving, and processing data. These methods are both manual and automated. The data can come from both internal sources (e.g., employees) and external sources (e.g., customers' online orders). Procedures and instructions will be coded into the AIS software. However, the procedures and instructions should also be "coded" into employees through documentation and training. The procedures and instructions must be followed consistently to be effective.

3. AIS Data

An AIS must have a database structure to store information, such as structured query language (SQL), which is a computer language commonly used for databases. SQL allows the data that is in the AIS to be manipulated and retrieved for reporting purposes. The AIS will also need various input screens for the diverse types of system users and data entry, as well as different output formats to meet the needs of different users and several types of information.

The data contained in an AIS is all the financial information pertinent to the organization's business practices. Any business data that impacts the company's finances should go into an AIS.

The type of data included in an AIS depends on the nature of the business, but it may consist of the following:

- Sales orders

- Customer billing statements

- Sales analysis reports

- Purchase requisitions

- Vendor invoices

- Check registers

- General ledger

- Inventory data

- Payroll information

- Timekeeping

- Tax information

The data can be used to prepare accounting statements and financial reports, including accounts receivable aging, depreciation or amortization schedules, a trial balance, and a profit and loss statement. Having all this data in one place—in the AIS—facilitates a business's record-keeping, reporting, analysis, auditing, and decision-making activities. For the data to be useful, it must be complete, accurate, and relevant.

On the other hand, examples of data that would not go into an AIS include memos, correspondence, presentations, and manuals. These documents might have a tangential relationship to the company's finances, but, excluding the standard footnotes, they are not really part of the company's financial record-keeping.

4. AIS Software

The software component of an AIS is the computer programs used to store, retrieve, process, and analyze the company's financial data. Before there were computers, an AIS was a manual, paper-based system, but today, most companies are using computer software as the basis of the AIS. Small businesses might use Intuit's QuickBooks or Sage's Sage 50 Accounting, but there are others. Small to mid-sized businesses might use SAP's Business One. Mid-sized and large businesses might use Microsoft's Dynamics GP, Sage Group's MAS 90, or MAS 200, Oracle's PeopleSoft, or Epicor Financial Management.

Quality, reliability, and security are key components of effective AIS software. Managers rely on the information it outputs to make decisions for the company, and they need high-quality information to make sound decisions.

AIS software programs can be customized to meet the unique needs of diverse types of businesses. If an existing program does not meet a company's needs, the software can also be developed in-house with substantial input from end-users or can be developed by a third-party company specifically for the organization. The system could even be outsourced to a specialized company.

For publicly traded companies, no matter what software program and customization options the business chooses, Sarbanes-Oxley regulations will dictate the structure of the AIS to some extent. This is because SOX regulations establish internal controls and auditing procedures with which public companies must comply.

5. IT Infrastructure

Information technology infrastructure is just a fancy name for the hardware used to operate the accounting information system. Most of these hardware items a business would need to have anyway and can include the following:

- Computers

- Mobile devices

- Servers

- Printers

- Surge protectors

- Routers

- Storage media

- A back-up power supply

In addition to cost, factors to consider in selecting hardware include speed, storage capability, and whether it can be expanded and upgraded.

Most importantly, the hardware selected for an AIS must be compatible with the intended software. Ideally, it would be not just compatible, but optimal—a clunky system will be much less helpful than a speedy one. One-way businesses can easily meet hardware and software compatibility requirements is by purchasing a turnkey system that includes both the hardware and the software that the business needs. Purchasing a turnkey system means, theoretically, that the business will get an optimal combination of hardware and software for its AIS.

A good AIS should also include a plan for maintaining, servicing, replacing, and upgrading components of the hardware system, as well as a plan for the disposal of broken and outdated hardware, so that sensitive data is destroyed.

6. Internal Controls

The internal controls of an AIS are the security measures it contains to protect sensitive data. These can be as simple as passwords or as complex as biometric identification. Biometric security protocols might include storing human characteristics that do not change over time, such as fingerprints, voice, and facial recognition.

An AIS must have internal controls to protect against unauthorized computer access and to limit access to authorized users, which includes some users inside the company. It must also prevent unauthorized file access by individuals who are allowed to access only select parts of the system.

An AIS contains confidential information belonging not just to the company but also to its employees and customers. This data may include:

- Social Security numbers

- Salary and personnel information

- Credit card numbers

- Customer information

- Company financial data

- Financial information of suppliers and vendors

All the data in an AIS should be encrypted, and access to the system should be logged and surveilled. System activity should be traceable as well.

An AIS also needs internal controls that protect it from computer viruses, hackers, and other internal and external threats to network security. It must also be protected from natural disasters and power surges that can cause data loss.

Real World Examples of Accounting Information Systems

A well-designed AIS allows a business to run smoothly on a day-to-day basis while a poorly designed AIS can hinder its operation. The third use for an AIS is that, when a business is in trouble, the data in its AIS can be used to uncover the story of what went wrong. The cases of WorldCom and Lehman Brothers provide two examples.

WorldCom

In 2002, WorldCom's internal auditors Eugene Morse and Cynthia Cooper used the company's AIS to uncover $4 billion in fraudulent expense allocations and other accounting entries. Their investigation led to the termination of CFO Scott Sullivan, as well as new legislation—section 404 of the Sarbanes-Oxley Act, which regulates companies' internal financial controls and procedures.

Lehman Brothers

When investigating the causes of Lehman's collapse, a review of its AIS and other data systems was a key component, along with document collection and review, plus witness interviews. The search for the causes of the company's failure "required an extensive investigation and review of Lehman's operating, trading, valuation, financial, accounting, and other data systems," according to the 2,200-page, nine-volume examiner's report.

Lehman's systems provide an example of how an AIS should not be structured. Examiner Anton R. Valukas' report states, "At the time of its bankruptcy filing, Lehman maintained a patchwork of over 2,600 software systems and applications... Many of Lehman's systems were arcane, outdated or non-standard."

The examiner decided to focus his efforts on the 96 systems that appeared most relevant. This examination required training, study, and trial and error just to learn how to use the systems.

Valukas' report also noted, "Lehman's systems were highly interdependent, but their relationships were difficult to decipher and not well-documented. It took extraordinary effort to untangle these systems to obtain the necessary information."

The Bottom Line

The six components of an AIS all work together to help key employees collect, store, manage, process, retrieve, and report their financial data. Having a well-developed and maintained accounting information system that is efficient and accurate is an indispensable component of a successful business.

Inventory Accounting
What Is Inventory Accounting?

Inventory accounting is the body of accounting that deals with valuing and accounting for changes in inventoried assets. A company's inventory typically involves goods in three stages of production: raw goods, in-progress goods, and finished goods that are ready for sale. Inventory accounting will assign values to the items in each of these three processes and record them as company assets. Assets are goods that will be of future value to the company, so they need to be accurately valued for the company to have a precise valuation.

Key Takeaways

- Inventory accounting determines the specific value of assets at certain stages in their development and production.

- This accounting method ensures an accurate representation of the value of all assets, companywide.

- Careful examination by a company of these values could lead to increased profit margins at each stage of the product.

Inventory items at any of the three production stages can change in value. Changes in value can occur for a number of reasons including depreciation, deterioration, obsolescence, change in customer taste, increased demand, decreased market supply, and so on. An accurate inventory accounting system will keep track of these changes to inventory goods at all three production stages and adjust company asset values and the costs associated with the inventory accordingly.

How Inventory Accounting Works

GAAP requires inventory to be properly accounted for according to a very particular set of standards, to limit the potential of overstating profit by understating inventory value. Profit is revenue minus costs. Revenue is generated by selling inventory. If the inventory value (or cost) is understated, then the profit associated with the sale of the inventory may be overstated. That can potentially inflate the company's valuation.

The other item the GAAP rules guard against is the potential for a company to overstate its value by overstating the value of inventory. Since inventory is an asset, it affects the overall value of the company. A company which is manufacturing or selling an outdated item might see a

96

decrease in the value of its inventory. Unless this is accurately captured in the company financials, the value of the company's assets and thus the company itself might be inflated.

Advantages of Inventory Accounting

The main advantage of inventory accounting is to have an accurate representation of the company's financial health. However, there are some additional advantages to keeping track of the value of items through their respective production stages. Namely, inventory accounting allows businesses to assess where they may be able to increase profit margins on a product at a particular place in that product's cycle.

This can be seen most prominently in products that require exceptional time or expense in secondary stages of production. Items such as pharmaceuticals, machinery, and technology are three products that require copious amounts of expense after their initial designing. By evaluating the value of the product at a certain stage⊠—such as clinical trials or transportation of the product⊠—a company can adjust the variables at that stage to keep the product value the same while increasing their profit margins by decreasing expenses.

Last In, First Out (LIFO)
What Is Last In, First Out (LIFO)?

Last in, first out (LIFO) is a method used to account for inventory that records the most recently produced items as sold first. Under LIFO, the cost of the most recent products purchased (or produced) are the first to be expensed as cost of goods sold (COGS), which means the lower cost of older products will be reported as inventory.

Two alternative methods of inventory-costing include first in, first out (FIFO), where the oldest inventory items are recorded as sold first, and the average cost method, which takes the weighted average of all units available for sale during the accounting period and then uses that average cost to determine COGS and ending inventory.

Key Takeaways

- Last in, first out (LIFO) is a method used to account for inventory.

- Under LIFO, the costs of the most recent products purchased (or produced) are the first to be expensed.

- LIFO is used only in the United States and governed by the accepted accounting principles (GAAP).

- Other methods to account for inventory include first in, first out (FIFO) and the average cost method.

- Using LIFO typically lowers net income but is tax advantageous when prices are rising.

Understanding Last In, First Out (LIFO)

Last in, first out (LIFO) is only used in the United States where all three inventory-costing methods can be used under generally accepted accounting principles (GAAP). The International Financial Reporting Standards (IFRS) forbids the use of the LIFO method.

Companies that use LIFO inventory valuations are typically those with large inventories, such as retailers or auto dealerships, which can take advantage of lower taxes (when prices are rising) and higher cash flows.

Many U.S. companies prefer to use FIFO though, because if a firm uses a LIFO valuation when it files taxes, it must also use LIFO when it reports financial results to shareholders, which lowers net income and, ultimately, earnings per share.

Last In, First Out (LIFO), Inflation, and Net Income

When there is zero inflation, all three inventory-costing methods produce the same result. But if inflation is high, the choice of accounting method can dramatically affect valuation ratios. FIFO, LIFO, and average cost have a different impact:

- FIFO provides a better indication of the value of ending inventory (on the balance sheet), but it also increases net income because inventory that might be several years old is used to value COGS. Increasing net income sounds good, but it can increase the taxes that a company must pay.

- LIFO is not a good indicator of ending inventory value because it may understate the value of inventory. LIFO results in lower net income (and taxes) because COGS is higher. However, there are fewer inventory write-downs under LIFO during inflation.

- Average cost produces results that fall somewhere between FIFO and LIFO.

If prices are decreasing, then the opposite of the above is true.

Example of Last In, First Out (LIFO)

Assume company A has 10 widgets. The first five widgets cost $100 each and arrived two days ago. The last five widgets cost $200 each and arrived one day ago. Based on the LIFO method of inventory management, the last widgets in are the first ones to be sold. Seven widgets are sold, but how much can the accountant record as a cost?

Each widget has the same sales price, so revenue is the same, but the cost of the widgets is based on the inventory method selected. Based on the LIFO method, the last inventory in is the first inventory sold. This means the widgets that cost $200 sold first. The company then sold two more of the $100 widgets. In total, the cost of the widgets under the LIFO method is $1,200, or five at $200 and two at $100. In contrast, using FIFO, the $100 widgets are sold first, followed by the $200 widgets. So, the cost of the widgets sold will be recorded as $900, or five at $100 and two at $200.

This is why in periods of rising prices, LIFO creates higher costs and lowers net income, which also reduces taxable income. Likewise, in periods of falling prices, LIFO creates lower costs and increases net income, which also increases taxable income.

First In, First Out (FIFO)
What Is First In, First Out (FIFO)?

First In, First Out, commonly known as FIFO, is an asset-management and valuation method in which assets produced or acquired first are sold, used, or disposed of first.

For tax purposes, FIFO assumes that assets with the oldest costs are included in the income statement's cost of goods sold (COGS). The remaining inventory assets are matched to the assets that are most recently purchased or produced.

Key Takeaways

- First In, First Out (FIFO) is an accounting method in which assets purchased or acquired first are disposed of first.

- FIFO assumes that the remaining inventory consists of items purchased last.

- An alternative to FIFO, LIFO is an accounting method in which assets purchased or acquired last are disposed of first.

- Often, in an inflationary market, lower, older costs are assigned to the cost of goods sold under the FIFO method, which results in a higher net income than if LIFO were used.

First In, First Out (FIFO)

Understanding First In, First Out (FIFO)

The FIFO method is used for cost flow assumption purposes. In manufacturing, as items progress to later development stages and as finished inventory items are sold, the associated costs with that product must be recognized as an expense. Under FIFO, it is assumed that the cost of inventory purchased first will be recognized first. The dollar value of total inventory decreases in this process because inventory has been removed from the company's ownership. The costs associated with the inventory may be calculated in several ways — one being the FIFO method.

Typical economic situations involve inflationary markets and rising prices. In this situation, if FIFO assigns the oldest costs to the cost of goods sold, these oldest costs will theoretically be priced lower than the most recent inventory purchased at current inflated prices. This lower expense results in higher net income. Also, because the newest inventory was purchased at higher prices, the ending inventory balance is inflated.

Example of FIFO

Inventory is assigned costs as items are prepared for sale. This may occur through the purchase of the inventory or production costs, through the purchase of materials, and utilization of labor. These assigned costs are based on the order in which the product was used, and for FIFO, it is based on what arrived first. For example, if 100 items were purchased for $10 and 100 more items were purchased next for $15, FIFO would assign the cost of the first item resold of $10. After 100 items were sold, the added cost of the item would become $15, regardless of any additional inventory purchases made.

The FIFO method follows the logic that to avoid obsolescence, a company would sell the oldest inventory items first and maintain the newest items in inventory. Although the actual inventory valuation method used does not need to follow the actual flow of inventory through a company, an entity must be able to support why it selected the use of a particular inventory valuation method.

Average Cost Method
What Is the Average Cost Method?

The average cost method assigns a cost to inventory items based on the total cost of goods purchased or produced in a period divided by the total number of items purchased or produced. The average cost method is also known as the weighted-average method.

Key Takeaways

- The average cost method is one of three inventory valuation methods, with the other two common methods being first in first out (FIFO) and last in first out (LIFO).

- The average cost method uses the weighted average of all inventories purchased in a period to assign value to cost of goods sold (COGS) as well as the cost of goods still available for sale.

- Once a company selects an inventory valuation method, it needs to remain consistent in its use to be compliant with accepted accounting principles (GAAP).

Click Play to Learn What the Average Cost Method Is

Understanding the Average Cost Method

Businesses that sell products to customers must deal with inventory, which is either bought from a separate manufacturer or produced by the company itself. Items previously in inventory that are sold off are recorded on a company's income statement as cost of goods sold (COGS). The COGS is an important figure for businesses, investors, and analysts as it is subtracted from sales revenue to determine gross margin on the income statement. To calculate the total cost of goods sold to consumers during a period, different companies use one of three inventory cost methods—first in first out (FIFO), last in first out (LIFO), or average cost method.

The average cost method uses a simple average of all similar items in inventory, regardless of purchase date, followed by a count of final inventory items at the end of an accounting period. Multiplying the average cost per item by the final inventory count gives the company a figure for the cost of goods available for sale at that point. The same average cost is also applied to the number of items sold in the previous accounting period to determine the cost of goods sold.

Example of the Average Cost Method

For example, consider the following inventory ledger for Sam's Electronics:

Purchase date	Number of items	Cost per unit	Total cost
01/01	20	$1,000	$20,000
01/18	15	$1,020	$15,300
02/10	30	$1,050	$31,500
02/20	10	$1,200	$12,000
03/05	25	$1,380	$34,500
Total	100		

Assume the company sold 72 units in the first quarter. The weighted-average cost is the total inventory purchased in the quarter, $113,300, divided by the total inventory count from the quarter, 100, for an average of $1,133 per unit. The cost of goods sold will be recorded as 72 units sold x $1,133 average cost = $81,576. The cost of goods available for sale, or inventory at the end of the period, will be the 28 remaining items still in inventory x $1,133 = $31,724.

Benefits of the Average Cost Method

The average cost method requires minimal labor to apply and is, therefore, the least expensive of all the methods. In addition to the simplicity of applying the average cost method, income cannot be as easily manipulated as with the other inventory costing methods. Companies that sell products that are indistinguishable from each other or that find it difficult to find the cost associated with individual units will prefer to use the average cost method. This also helps when there are large volumes of related items moving through inventory, making it time-consuming to track each individual item.

Special Considerations

One of the core aspects of U.S. accepted accounting principles (GAAP) is consistency. The consistency principle requires a company to adopt an accounting method and follow it consistently from one accounting period to another. For example, businesses that adopt the average cost method need to continue to use this method for future accounting periods. This principle is in place for the ease of financial statement users so that figures on the financials can be compared year over year. A company that changes its inventory costing method must highlight the change in its footnotes to the financial statements.

Now that you have an insightful look into accounting, your ahead of most people in business. We wish you the best and see you at the bank.

CPSIA information can be obtained
at www.ICGtesting.com
Printed in the USA
LVHW072327150422
716318LV00001B/1